In the
TRENCHES

In the TRENCHES

A Teacher's Defense of Public Education

Dennis Fermoyle

Beaver's Pond Press, Inc.
Edina, Minnesota

ISBN-13: 978-1-59298-121-2
ISBN-10: 1-59298-121-6

Library of Congress Catalog Number: 2005931403

Printed in the United States of America

Second Printing: June 2006

09 08 07 06   5 4 3 2

Beaver's Pond Press, Inc.

7104 Ohms Lane, Suite 216
Edina, MN 55439
(952) 829-8818
www.BeaversPondPress.com

To order, visit *www.BookHouseFulfillment.com*
or call 1-800-901-3480. Reseller discounts available.

*To the public school teachers who do their best
and make our students' lives better,
and to the public school students who do their best
and make all of our lives better.*

Contents

Introduction

I have been a teacher and coach in public schools for thirty-one years, and I've loved doing both. I enjoy the challenge of most aspects of my job and, believe it or not, I am not looking forward to retirement. When people say they like teaching or coaching, they usually give very noble and unselfish reasons. I have more than one reason for enjoying what I do, and while I suppose a couple of those reasons are somewhat noble, the biggest reason I like teaching is that so many of the kids make me feel so good. More than anything else, they make me feel important—like I'm somebody who really matters. I know that as a teacher, I'm supposed to do what I can to make my students feel that way, but I don't think I can really ever give them the feeling they give me.

I have had a lot of positive experiences in my classroom over the years. Groups of students have often come into my room just to hang around before classes start and during lunch hours because they like being there and enjoy my company. I've had students tell me they like my class, that they like it when I lecture (amazing but true!), and that they like the way a lesson has been set up. I've received Teacher of the Year and Coach of the Year awards, and last, but certainly not least, I've had high school girls tell me I look like Richard Gere. That makes me feel a lot better than when my wife tells me that she thinks I look like Stan Laurel.

My teaching career hasn't been a bed of roses, however. I've had my share of negative experiences, and I don't know any teachers who haven't. I've had parents complain to administrators about me, and I've even had powerful members of my community demand that I be fired. I've had students blatantly defy me, sleep during my lectures, try to cheat their way through my class, and call me an asshole to my face. During my first week at the school where I now teach, I had a very petite, sixteen-year-old female student tell me politely that her father had refused to sign a letter I had sent home explaining how I did things, and he had asked her to tell me that I could take my system and "shove it where the sun doesn't shine."

One particularly frustrating thing about being a teacher is that everyone thinks that they know how to do my job. Very few people would ever presume to tell a doctor how to do his job, and not many would ever dare to tell a lawyer how to do hers. Two of my sons are in the computer field, and I don't understand what they do, even when they explain it to me slowly. Although I'm no rocket scientist, I think I have at least an average amount of computer literacy, so I'm pretty sure they don't have to worry too much about their next door neighbors telling them how to do their jobs. But almost everyone has gone to school, so just about everyone has an opinion about teaching and how it should be done. And, as is usually true for people who have an opinion about how to do something that they don't have to do themselves, the vast majority of them think it is a lot easier to do than it actually is.

While one layperson after another seems to have an opinion about how I should do my job, there is also an endless stream of "experts" on the subject. TV talk shows are absolutely overflowing with them. All politicians running for office are experts. If you don't believe me, just ask them. University professors are experts. Superintendents of gigantic school districts are experts. The judges who have made decisions forcing teachers to tolerate things in classrooms that would never be tolerated in courtrooms are experts. Former Secretaries of Education, such as William Bennett, are experts. Anyone who has written a book or an article or done a study and spent time observing a classroom is an expert. Some of these experts make policy, and some of these experts are listened to very closely by those who make policy. Yet, when I see and listen to these experts on TV and read what they have to say in articles and books, I find it so obvious that many of them don't have the slightest idea about what it is actually like to teach in a public school classroom.

I have three basic reasons for writing this book. First, I think people might be interested in learning what it is actually like to be a teacher in a public school today. Second, I think there is room for an opinion on education issues from someone who actually does it. At this point I'd love to impress you by rattling off the several degrees and honors I have and the titles of the articles I've written, but I can't. In fact, there really isn't anything in particular that would make me stand out from many other teachers. I do have a Masters Degree, but I've known a lot of teachers without advanced degrees who do a better job than many who have them, so that really isn't anything to get that excited about. I'm just a regular teacher.

But maybe that gives my opinions value that they wouldn't have if I had all those other honors and degrees. During my career I've taught basic classes made up entirely of kids who had low aptitude in a subject, and I've taught advanced placement classes made up entirely of kids who were bound for college. I've had classes to which I dared not turn my back and students who couldn't name our first president, but I've also had fantastic classes and fantastic students, including one young woman who earned a perfect score on her SAT. As a hockey coach, I've had some terrible teams, including one that went winless through an entire season, and I've had players who couldn't skate backwards without falling down. But I've also had teams that won state championships, and several players who have earned Division I college scholarships, one who made it all the way to the National Hockey League. There aren't many things about teaching and coaching in public high schools that I haven't seen since I truly have lived my last thirty-one years in the trenches. I really do know what it's like.

I don't teach in New York City. In fact, I don't teach in any big city at all. I teach in a small town in northern Minnesota, and when I read about education in some of those large metropolitan areas, I feel like I'm reading about a foreign country. I am in no way dismissing the experiences and problems that take place in those areas, but there are a lot of schools like mine and a lot of teachers like me. In fact, I suspect that my situation might be representative of more teachers in more schools than those of teachers in New York City. People in my situation certainly need to be cognizant of what's going on in places like New York, but maybe the public and the people in those larger schools can gain from knowing what goes on in our schools, too.

Finally, my most important reason for writing this book is to give public education the defense it deserves. With the exception of a few short years spent in college, I have been involved in K-12 education ever since I was five years old. For the past several years, I have been reading horror stories about terrible teachers and terrible schools, but the teachers and schools with which I am familiar are working harder and doing more creative things than ever before. Although I am aware that problems do exist, I still strongly believe in public schools.

This book will include five arguments that have too often been ignored in contemporary discussions about public education:

1. There are many public schools and public school teachers that are doing a far better job than they are given credit for. Many public school students do very well and go on to be successful in college and in their careers, but this fact is largely ignored by the critics of public education. The conventional wisdom that American public schools are "failing" is unfair, and yet it threatens to become a self-fulfilling prophecy.

2. We have been hearing a great deal about public school students who perform poorly. Far too much of the responsibility for this is being placed on the schools and teachers, and far too little is being placed on parents, our culture, and especially the low-performing students themselves.

3. Policy makers have been oblivious to the very important effect that students have on each other. Court rulings and legislation over the last forty years have made it nearly impossible for schools to remove disruptive and apathetic students, and now public policy is encouraging motivated students to leave. This is a recipe for disaster for public education.

4. The educational reforms that have been and are presently being forced upon public schools and teachers are not the answers to our problems.

5. We can significantly improve public education by doing two basic things: increasing the power of teachers in their classrooms, and increasing the power of principals in their schools.

Since I'm a product of public education, and since it's been the source of my income for all of my adult life, it would be hard for me to say that I am unbiased on the subject. Nevertheless, I think it's unarguable that public education has served our nation very well over our history. It truly has been "the great equalizer" that has made it possible for the "rags to riches" myth to become reality for an amazing number of people. Contrary to what many media reports would have us believe, it is still doing that for many kids today, and my hope is that it can continue to do that in the future. As I sit here in front of my ten-year-old Macintosh computer, I dream of making a small contribution to the continued success of public education. Given the challenges it faces, though, it might seem that I am engaged in a hopeless cause. But I am a public school teacher, and if there's one thing I've learned from that, it's that sometimes hopeless causes aren't so hopeless after all.

NOTE: All of the incidents and situations described in this book are true, but the names of many of the people used in describing them have been changed, and other alterations have been made to protect the innocent—and the guilty.

Beating Up on Public Education

A number of years ago I was watching a discussion on CNN between guests with opposing views about the value of a "poverty tour" that President Clinton was taking. This wasn't a calm discussion of the facts. It was one of those shout-a-thons that have become increasingly popular in our culture and, as anyone who has watched any of them knows, there usually are definite winners and losers. In this case, one of the participants was clearly losing. He was continually on the defensive, and was actually pushed to the point of stuttering and stammering when he suddenly blurted out, "Our public education system is a national disgrace!"

Bringing the subject of public education into a discussion about poverty may not seem unreasonable but, based on the content of that conversation, this comment was totally out of the blue. It was obvious that the gentleman who made this proclamation was losing his argument, and he was looking for something to say that no one could possibly refute. And what could be better for that purpose than to slam public education?

Although this incident took place on CNN, it wouldn't be fair to say that this network goes out of its way to bash public education. But then there's Fox News. Fox News advertises itself as fair and balanced, but I've gotten the impression that the network is just a tad conservative when it comes to politics, and conservatives have not been friendly to public education. No one demonstrates this more clearly than Fox news anchor, Brit Hume.

If I were to give someone the title "King of the Public Education Bashers," Brit would definitely get the honor. On his nightly political news program, *Special Report with Brit Hume,* he often runs stories that seem to point out that public schools in America are doing a terrible job. One night he'll have something about a teacher who's done something incredibly stupid in some small town in Texas. A few nights later, he'll report about a principal or school board that has made a seemingly mindless decision in some medium sized city in Illinois. At the end of these kinds of pieces, Brit faces the camera with a knowing and disgusted look that seems to say, "There they go again!"

The discussion I saw on CNN and the pieces Brit Hume is so fond of running are typical of the media's portrayal of public education over the last twenty to thirty years. This has been the case especially since the National Commission on Excellence in Education published *A Nation at Risk* in 1983. The report claimed, "If an unfriendly foreign power had imposed our schools upon us we would have regarded it as an act of war."[1] Since that time, the media has adopted a similarly alarmist theme. The media has consistently made it sound as though public education is doing nothing right, and doing everything wrong.

Countless books have come out criticizing public education, and the criticisms range from the contradictory to the ridiculous. James Loewen, in his book *Lies My Teacher Told Me,* blasts our schools by arguing convincingly that they are teaching too many facts and are not nearly progressive enough. E.D. Hirsch, in his book *The Schools We Need,* blasts our public schools by arguing convincingly that they are focusing on ridiculous progressive reforms and not teaching enough facts. In an e-mail item that was circulating shortly after the 9/11 terrorist attacks, Anne Graham, when asked why God would allow something like that to happen, answered by explaining that because we no longer allow God in public schools, it was our fault. And last, but certainly not least, Peter Brimelow begins his book *The Worm in the Apple* by telling the world that teachers are fat.[2]

1. National Commission on Excellence in Education, (1983). A nation at risk: the imperative for educational reform. Washington, D.C.: U.S. Government Printing Office, 5

2. Brimelow, P. (2003). The worm in the apple: how the teacher unions are destroying American education. New York: HarperCollins, 1

Anyone who has paid attention to public discussions about education in America for the last fifteen or twenty years would have to be amazed that our country hasn't completely fallen apart. In 1991, the United States was in a recession and it appeared that nations like Japan, whose economy was going along like gangbusters, were making huge gains on us. At that time, the talking heads on TV explained this by pointing to the American education system. "Our public schools are terrible," they said. "No wonder we can't compete with the Japanese." There was much made of the fact that Japanese students attend school for several more days a year than do American students, giving the general impression that people coming out of the Japanese education system were clearly superior to our graduates. It was at about this time that Michael Crichton wrote *Rising Sun*. Crichton's book, though a great story, was disturbing because he made a very convincing case that Japan was about to take over the United States economically. But then what happened? Japan's economy went into the tank for the rest of the decade, the United States economy recovered, and we enjoyed a prosperity that became the envy of the world. How could we do that given all those poor illiterate fools our schools had been producing? The critics must be stumped.

Sometimes, the way we are blamed for things defies common sense. For example, a few years ago, a letter to the editor appeared in our local newspaper in which the writer blamed our school system for a number of teen pregnancies that had "occurred" that year. Those pregnancies, the writer said, were all the fault of our school's sex education program. She implied that if teenage girls were getting pregnant, the teachers who ran the program must not have been doing their jobs. I know, however, that most of the girls to whom the writer was referring were reasonably intelligent academically, and when it came to street sense, they were more than reasonably intelligent. Could the woman who wrote this letter honestly have thought that those girls didn't know how they could get pregnant? Or could she possibly have thought that they got pregnant because they weren't aware of birth control methods? I think I know why those girls got pregnant and why their partners got them pregnant, and these reasons have nothing to do with what they did or didn't learn in their sex education classes.

Written by some woman in northern Minnesota, this letter hardly indicates a media frenzy, but you hear that type of thing all the time. Recently, while watching *The O'Reilly Factor*, I saw a woman being grilled about the high rate of teenage pregnancies among African-American girls. She explained this by saying that students needed more education. Although she wasn't explicitly blaming public schools, she clearly implied that schools were failing to do something.

Sometimes the criticisms of public education involve comparisons to public education in "the good old days." Sol Stern, in his book *Breaking Free,* refers to the 1950s as "the golden era of the New York City public schools,"[3] and I'm sure many people around the country view schools in their communities the same way: if only we could get back to doing things the way we did in the fifties! I'd like some of the people who feel that way to tell that to my wife. She attended an elementary school in a supposedly topflight school district in a Twin Cities suburb in the late 1950's, and suffered a series of ear infections that caused her to have a severe hearing problem. In fact, her hearing was so bad that she didn't know that walking on grass made sound until after a surgery she had when she was fourteen. Yet, she never received any help for her problem from that "great" school system, and was even spanked once by a substitute teacher in front of the class because she couldn't say her name correctly. Ah, for the good old days!

Comparisons are also made between our K-12 public education and colleges and universities. I've heard public education critics refer to America's higher education system as the envy of the world. They say that our public schools should try to be more like them. I have three sons who attended public schools and then went on to attend colleges, two to different state universities in Minnesota and one to a private university in Florida. All three of them say that their worst teachers were certain professors they had in college. College students are able to get a good education despite this, in part because other professors are excellent, and in part because students are often highly motivated. If college students don't have enough motivation, they'll end up dropping out, and nobody minds. If a high school student isn't motivated and drops out, it's considered a failure on the school's part.

3. Stern, S. (2003). *Breaking free.* San Francisco, CA: Encounter Books, 5

There are times when critics make suggestions about how we can improve our public schools that are almost laughable. *Lies My Teacher Told Me*, by James Loewen, is one of the best books I've ever read; it is a great resource for my American history courses because it has an abundance of interesting stories that I can use in my classes. But providing stories for history teachers is not Loewen's major purpose; attacking the way history has been taught in America is. As valuable as I find *Lies My Teacher Told Me*, some of Loewen's most important conclusions leave me shaking my head. He begins his book by berating textbook publishers and teachers for making history classes boring, but then suggests that teachers liven our classes by teaching students that Woodrow Wilson invaded Haiti.[4] Hey, that ought to really grab those kids! After that, he argues that Africans *might* have visited the Americas before Columbus, and that we'd have students "on the edge of their seats" if we only taught them this.[5] Now, as someone who is interested in almost anything involving American history, I'll concede that this point is interesting. Although I question how strong an influence this piece of information would have, I also understand the idea that including more in our history classes about the contributions of Africans might do something for the self-esteem of young blacks. But anyone who says that something like this would have students on the edges of their seats sounds a lot more like a college professor than a high school teacher.

Loewen may have read a lot of books and even observed high school classrooms, but to an actual classroom teacher, like me, he appears clueless when it comes to the practicalities of teaching high school students. Nevertheless, whenever someone from a university setting says something about any level of education, the public tends to take it as the authoritative word on the subject.

A few years ago ABC aired a news piece about a study that criticized suspensions and expulsions in public schools. In ABC's report, a pretty, young college professor and a very intelligent looking young man, both of whom had been involved in the study, were interviewed in their fashionable offices, and they gave a list of seemingly compelling reasons why students shouldn't be suspended or expelled. Then ABC showed a haggard looking principal being interviewed about why her inner-city mid-

4. Loewen, J. W. (1995). *Lies my teacher told me*. New York: The New Press, 15
5. Ibid., 40

dle school had such a high suspension rate. She simply said that they suspended students so they could have a safe learning environment in their school. There is no question that the young people from the college came away looking more impressive and smarter in those interviews, but that principal was the only one who ever actually had to deal with disruptive students. As a teacher, I know that we are supposed to love and value every child, but I have had the experience of dealing with disruptive kids in my classroom who showed no desire for an education. To be perfectly honest, I find some of them hard to love. If I had to choose from the people on that news piece who I wanted running my school, I'd pick that haggard looking principal in her dumpy old office any day.

Very often critics use anecdotes and statistics from certain large cities and certain states to paint a general picture of the status of public education in the United States. Maybe things are as bad in New York City as Sol Stern says they are. Maybe some of those teachers in California are as ignorant as Peter Brimelow says they are. Maybe things in Washington, D.C., Milwaukee and Cleveland are so bad that allowing families to use vouchers makes sense in those places. It's hard for me to make the argument that they're not because I have no direct familiarity with those places.

What angers me, and what I know is unfair, is the inference made by the experts familiar with the situations in those places that public education is terrible "in America." It's not just terrible in New York City or Washington, D.C., but according to these implications it's terrible in Warroad, Minnesota, too. Well, I'm here to tell you that it's not terrible in Warroad, Minnesota.

I have taught and coached at Warroad High School for sixteen years. During those sixteen years, I have found that any student who comes and takes classes here will get a good education as long as she has a desire to learn and a willingness to make an honest effort. If she wants to get into a college, she will almost certainly be able to do so, and she will almost certainly be able to be successful there. We have many former students attending large state universities, such as those of Minnesota and North Dakota, and many others going to state and private colleges in our region. We've also had kids go on to places like Harvard, Yale, Princeton, Stanford, the Air Force Academy and other prestigious universities around the country. Some of these former students are now doctors, some are lawyers, some are bankers, some are computer programmers, some are biologists, some are chemical engineers, some work in large corporations, and some have opened their own small businesses. We also have a number of former students who have become teachers and coaches, others who have become pharmacists, and still others who have become nurses.

The accomplishments of these students do not set our school apart from other public schools. Like most teachers, I want to believe there is something special about my school, but I have to admit that there is no evidence to suggest that we are in a league of our own. I know that Roseau High School, our neighbor to the west, could list its students' impressive accomplishments as proudly as we can, and so could Lake of the Woods High School, our neighbor to the east. I think it's safe to assume that there are thousands of public schools throughout the United States with hundreds of thousands of teachers who are doing good things, just as we are. If public education is as miserable as so many of our critics contend, how in the world could so many of our kids have done so well?

I will argue in this book that most public school teachers are competent, work hard, and do a good job. I cannot argue, however, that we do a good job defending ourselves against attacks by critics. Sadly, many of us have bought into the idea that it is all our fault when students perform poorly academically, and there are times when even we can't wait to jump on our critics' bandwagon.

A couple of years ago, I attended a workshop in which the presenter, a teacher-turned-college-professor, told the story of a sixth grade girl with whom he had worked. The girl had refused to do a required assignment. The presenter said he tried everything he could to encourage her, but she wouldn't do it. Finally, he asked her why she wouldn't just give it a try. She told him, "Because if I try, it won't be very good, and I'll be a failure; but if I don't try, then you're the failure." The presenter closed this story by saying with a look of sadness on his face, "And you know, she was right."

No story I've ever heard illustrates the masochism of teachers better than this one. How could this intelligent man come to this ridiculous conclusion? He provided that girl with the opportunity to learn, and he did everything he could to motivate her. He did everything a good teacher should do. He was not the problem; the problem was a student who refused to try. As harsh as this may sound, that little girl had it backwards. Her teacher was not the failure; she was.

Conventional wisdom holds that if a student is doing poorly, the school is doing something wrong. When someone tells a story like that of this little girl, we are all supposed to nod our heads and agree. And many of the teachers in that workshop did just that. After all, we hear this type of thing from public officials; books are written about it, we read it in the newspapers, and, most importantly, the talking heads on TV have told us it is so. Talk about rote learning!

Do we have some kids who perform miserably at Warroad High School? You bet! But isn't it logical to conclude that this might not be the fault of the school and the teachers when so many other students, like the ones described earlier—students with varying abilities—are able to do so well. Perhaps the biggest problem in public education today is the accepted idea that responsibility for learning lies with somebody other than the student.

Does all of this mean that there are no valid criticisms of public education? Definitely not. In fact, I'll be making a number of them myself. Am I saying that no one should ever criticize a particular teacher or teachers as a group? Not at all! And once again, I've got a few criticisms of my own. After all, I am a teacher, and nobody criticizes more than teachers.

Criticism can and should be a good thing. But in order for that to be the case, the criticism has to have some constructive purpose. Ideally, criticism helps someone to know how they can improve. Some of the criticism public education faces today has "correction" as a goal, but a lot of it—like the tidbits Brit Hume likes to dish out—serves no useful purpose. While some of the criticism is valid, much of it, like blaming public schools for teenage pregnancies, is not, and much of it centers around things that those of us inside public school buildings have only limited power to change.

I am so touchy about the barrage of criticism of public schools because I see a real danger in this criticism making public education in America worse instead of better. It can do that by leading us to give in to counterproductive reform ideas that defy common sense. We have already done some of that, but that's not my biggest fear. The ultimate result of so much criticism could be to turn public schools into holding cells for those young people in our society who have no hopes, no dreams, and no drive.

I teach in a good school. Nevertheless, in recent years, with all the criticism of public schools, a growing number of good parents in our community who care about their kids' education have concluded that we aren't good enough. As a consequence, we have lost some of our motivated young people to private schools and to homeschooling. We still have a good school, but we're not as good as we would be if we had those kids.

The most critical need in our public schools today is for good parents who really think education is important to have enough confidence in us to trust us with their children. Good parents who send their kids to public schools may not know it, but they are performing a service to their communities and to our nation. If we have enough kids from those families, our public schools are going to be just fine. But if more and more of those good parents become convinced that public schools are too inadequate for their kids, then that perception will increasingly become reality. And that would be a national tragedy.

The Key Ingredient

What makes a school good? If you asked that question of a number of people many of them would first say "good teachers." Another common answer might be "parental involvement," which seems to be very much in vogue today. Some might refer to having a state of the art building and equipment. There has been considerable effort made in recent years to make sure that students have access to computers and the Internet. There are also people who would probably answer the question with one word, "Discipline!" They would point to the success of many low-budget Catholic schools as evidence of what an emphasis on discipline can do. Finally, teachers' unions and many Democratic politicians might answer with flowery statements, but those statements would probably also come down to one word, "Money!"

All of these are reasonable answers, but something very important is missing, and it is something that is neglected consistently by public education critics and educational reformers. The missing element is good students. Thirty-one years of teaching seventh through twelfth graders has convinced me that the single most important factor in determining how much learning takes place in a high school classroom is the make-up of the students. In other words, how many motivated students are there in that classroom? How many average students are there? And how many disruptive and apathetic ones? This factor is so important because of the effect that students have on each other. If two or three highly motivated students are added to a class, other students in the class will learn more. On the other hand, if a disruptive student or a couple of apathetic ones are added to the mix, the learning of other students in the class will suffer. Since I've never taught in an elementary school, I can't say with certainty that this is the most important factor there, but I'm willing to bet that it's one of the top two or three.

I know that, coming from a teacher, this sounds like a cop-out. After all, aren't we the ones who are supposed to turn kids into good students? We definitely play a role in that, but studies have shown that the most important factors in determining which students turn out to be successful are actually the families and the neighborhoods the kids come from.[6]

I'm not saying teachers aren't important. We certainly are, and I think we should be held more accountable within our school districts than we are. Principals and other administrators are also important, and they should be held accountable, too. Nevertheless, I am convinced that many schools can be mediocre in those two areas, while an amazing amount of education can take place if they have enough highly motivated students. On the other hand, there can be wonderful and caring teachers and a fantastic administration, but if there are a large number of unmotivated kids who see school as a social event and a place for doing outrageous things, quality education just isn't going to happen.

If Only They Were All Like This!

In the public schools in which I've taught, most of my classes have had a normal mix of students. An average class would consist of some highly motivated students, a couple of apathetic ones, and the majority somewhere in between. Every once in a while, though, I'll luck out and get a class in which an unusually high number of kids are well up on the motivation scale. It is pure pleasure to teach those classes. I walk into the room and see smiling faces, and those smiling faces are the result of the students' happiness at seeing me and being in the class. Students come to class having done the assignments, so when I bring up a subject, almost every one of them knows what I'm talking about. When I ask questions,

6. Rose, P., Glazer, P., Glazer, M.(1989). *Sociology: understandingsociety.* Needham Heights, MA: Prentice Hall, Inc., 160

hands shoot up, and the biggest problem is keeping students from blurting out answers before I call on someone. Not only do they answer my questions, but they ask me questions because they are actually interested. When we have class discussions, they get excited and even show some emotion when they argue about the subjects with which we're dealing. When someone says something funny, it's not meant to hurt anyone, and if there's a lot of laughter, I don't have to worry that this is going to cause the class to reel out of control. This is not a fantasy: I really have had classes like this, and if every class were like that, I'd never retire. Never!

Bad Apples

But not every class is like that. Not by a long shot. One night, I had the TV on and wasn't really paying attention to it until I heard one of the talking heads say that he wished he could go into some of our inner-city schools and fire all the teachers. No, it wasn't Brit—he must have had the night off—but it must have been one of his soul mates. Obviously this "expert" wanted to place the blame for the poor performance of inner-city students squarely on the shoulders of those teachers. Well, that "expert" should fire those teachers only if he were one of the people replacing them.

I've never taught in an inner-city school, so I can only imagine what it is like. But just being aware of the social problems existing in those areas and hearing about some things that happen in those schools makes me certain that it's not something I'd want to try anytime soon.

I have spent my career in two working-class towns in northern Minnesota, Mt. Iron and Warroad. We've had our share of social problems, such as broken marriages, one-parent families, some crime, some drugs, some alcoholism, and a few just plain horrible parents. With such conditions, there will be some students who are challenging to have in class, and a few who are disruptive and almost impossible to handle. But the social problems that exist in the communities where I've taught pale in comparison to those in which some others are trying to teach, and I know how fortunate I am. It doesn't take a sociologist to figure out that increased social problems in a community mean more unmotivated and disruptive students.

Every year I get one or two really disruptive students in my classes. Having one of these kids in class can be a nightmare, and that one student can significantly cut the learning that takes place among the other students in a classroom. This is something that I sense "experts" do not understand, and they also seem not to understand that public school teachers don't have very much power in dealing with such disruptive students.

In *Breaking Through*, Sol Stern glowingly describes a Catholic school he visited. In this school, any violence results in automatic expulsion and, according to an interview he had with a student, it's necessary to work hard in order to stay in the school.[7] This means, I assume, that a student could be kicked out if she doesn't make a genuine effort. I wish we had that power in public schools, but we don't. I have had students removed from my class, but this required that I document a number of the students' blatant incidents of misbehavior, and show that the students were doing so poorly that they had virtually no chance of passing the class. If I could show one part of this requirement, but not the other, I'd probably be stuck with the troubled student. In my experience, then, the only way a teacher can get a student removed from a class is if the student just doesn't care. If the student wants to remain in the class, even if it's just to disrupt it, that student will probably be able to stay.

In the movies and on TV, disruptive students are often portrayed as witty, cute, and fundamentally goodhearted. In the 1970s sitcom *Welcome Back Kotter*, Gabe Kaplan played a teacher in charge of a classroom of these kids affectionately known as "the sweathogs." The sweathogs were the kids whom no other teachers wanted in their classrooms, but the kindhearted and caring Mr. Kotter showed us that they were really wonderful kids who just needed to be understood.

In reality, most disruptive students are mean, sneaky, rebellious game players. Many of them have made careers out of taking advantage of "understanding teachers." The disruptive student doesn't want to be told what to do by any adult no matter how politely it is done, yet his behavior always needs correcting by the teacher. When the bell rings, he will never be at his desk, so he has to be told to sit down. When he is told to do that, he will do it, but not right away, and when he finally saunters

7. Stern, *Breaking free*, 206

back to his desk, it is at a defiantly slow pace. If a classroom activity is going on, he will do whatever he knows he's not supposed to do. If a class is working in groups, the disruptive student will be talking to people from groups other than his own. If a class discussion is going on, he will be talking to anyone who will listen. Tell him to stop, and he will—for about a minute. Then he will be talking to someone else. If he gets into the classroom while the teacher is in the hallway, something bad will surely happen, or something will disappear. The game of the disruptive student is to go as far as possible and get away with as much as possible without actually getting kicked out of the class.

My first tactic in dealing with disruptive students is to talk to them one on one, and explain to them that I am not the enemy. I tell them that I'm not personally concerned with having power over them, but that I've got a job to do. If I allow them to do whatever they want, then I have to let everyone else in the class do that, and we just can't operate that way. I tell them I want them to enjoy the class and be successful in it, but they have to behave reasonably, and listen to me when I tell them to do something. Fermoyle—master psychologist!

Sometimes this works for about a day. Eventually, my strategy becomes one of documenting any of their actions that are worth documenting, kicking them out of class whenever I can justify it, and lobbying the principal to remove the student from my class, either for the semester or the year. That usually can't be done, and when it can be, it takes a lot of valuable time. In the meantime, my other students are stuck with someone who is damaging their education, and I'm stuck with someone who makes it difficult, if not impossible, to do my job the way I want to do it.

During my first year in Warroad, I had a young man who had some sort of chronic sinus problem. His eyes were always red, and his nose was always congested. That student mastered a trick that I've never seen before or since. In fact, I've never actually seen it at all because he would only perform it between passing bells when I was out of the room. He began his nifty trick by blowing his nose into an open hand. He would then throw that hand up as hard as he could, and smack down on that arm with his opposite hand causing the mucous to shoot up to the ceiling, where it would hang ominously above his head. He didn't seem to mind. All I do is teach social studies, so it's tough for me to compete for the other students' attention when I've got someone who can come up with a performance like that. Although that particular stunt was not actually done during class time, it accurately reflected the student's attitude toward school in general. He was not a joy to have in class, and he definitely made it more difficult for me to do my job. Compared to some other disruptive kids I've had, however, he was relatively harmless.

A few years ago I had a student named Sam, who had returned to our school after having been sent away for threatening to kill his parents. My understanding is that he came back to our school, at least in part, because the correctional institutions to which he was sent could do nothing with him. Great reason to send someone back to school, isn't it? Sam was a fairly bright sixteen-year-old who hated authority, and he consistently went out of his way to do the opposite of what his teachers wanted. His game was to try to force the teacher to react when provoked. He might just openly talk to another student while something was being presented, or he might make various noises. A teacher who asked him to stop talking or to be quiet could never be sure of Sam's reaction, but it probably wasn't going to be obedience. Every minute—no exaggeration—that I had this very disturbed young man in my class, I was faced with making decisions about how to deal with him, because he was doing something disruptive all the time. Should I react to what he just did? Am I better off ignoring it? If I react, how will he react, and how should I react to his reaction?

One day Sam came into my class and didn't sit down. He just stood by his desk. Once again, I had to ask myself, should I react? That time I thought to myself, "He's obviously playing a game with me; if I ignore him, maybe he'll get tired of standing and just sit down." After a couple of minutes, he did. I later found out that Sam had done the exact same thing in his English class, and that teacher had asked him to sit down. She had taken the bait! He responded by asking why, and she had to explain to him why he had to sit down. That may not have been so bad, but she ended up having to go through the same routine every day for the next couple of weeks. In that situation, I made the right decision, but that wasn't always the case. Sam also discussed with other students which teachers he'd like to kill, and we couldn't do anything about it because it was all hearsay, and Columbine hadn't happened yet. Today (and why should we be surprised?) that former student is in prison.

Before I go on, I should say that I recognize that someone reading this might think, "Why didn't you just throw him out of class whenever he did something disruptive?" I did that more than once, but like every other teacher who had Sam, I felt like I had to be careful. When his mother sent him back to school after his two-year stint in the training centers, she asked for a meeting with his teachers and the principal, demanding that we treat her son fairly and not discriminate against him based on his history. It was clear that she assumed we would not treat him fairly, and it was also clear that she understood *he had a right to an education*, and we had better provide it. When I deal with a disruptive student, I know that any action I take in dealing with him may come under attack, and this is especially true when the student has a mother like that. Even if I personally know that taking a particular action in dealing with a student is reasonable, I had better not take that action unless I know that I can convince someone who wasn't there, like a judge, that I have done the right thing. So that was the situation with Sam, at least until dear ol' Mom kicked him out of her house again.

Most students behave well, in part, because they don't want to get "in trouble." They fear simple consequences like being scolded, or a call to their parents, or having to serve detention, or worse yet, being suspended. Truly disruptive students have no fear of any of these things. When I was in high school, there was also the possibility that a teacher might actually get physical with a student, like slap him, for example. Obviously, that is not a factor anymore. In fact, in the last fifteen years I have actually had two separate incidents in which male students did something blatantly wrong in front of me, and when I turned their way with a look of obvious displeasure, they looked defiantly back at me and said, "If you hit me, I'll sue you." I didn't know whether to laugh or cry.

If you've never taught, you have no idea how frustrating it is to have a really disruptive student in your classroom. When you have to focus so much on one troublemaker, it becomes very difficult to do your job well for the other students. I teach American history. I want the kids to focus on American history, but that becomes impossible when a disruptive student is doing things that can't be ignored. In many classes—mine included—the best learning takes place when there is a lot of give and take, and that requires an open environment in which the teacher doesn't feel the necessity of maintaining overly tight control. Having to deal with one disruptive student, especially if that student is funny—and some of them really are—makes it impossible for a teacher to allow that open environment. And that's with only one disruptive student.

Every few years, I'll get a class that has more than one disruptive kid in it. If there are two or three really disruptive students in a class, they will almost always drag along a couple of other kids with them, so rather than there being two or three problem students, there will end up being five or six. These five or six kids will compete with each other to see who can get away with the most outrageous behavior. Teaching a class like that is a miserable experience for me, and it's a miserable experience for any kids in the class who want to learn something.

I can only imagine what it must be like to teach in a school in which there are three, four or more disruptive students in class, after class, after class. From what I've heard about inner-city schools, I think it's reasonable to assume that teachers in them face this situation with some frequency. There are an inordinate number of social problems in the inner-cities, so it's safe to say that their schools will have increased behavior problems. It seems to me that it's a miracle if any learning takes place in some of those schools. There are probably teachers in those schools who couldn't get jobs anywhere else, but some others are probably there because they really believe they can make a positive difference in an unbelievably difficult situation. They should be given medals, not more abuse from self-appointed experts on TV.

Good Apples

Just as disruptive students can severely curtail the education in a public school classroom, good students can greatly enhance it. I have coached hockey ever since I became a teacher, and every parent or follower of any one of our teams has understood that if one of our best players is lost, the team is going to suffer. Very few people seem to understand that this is also the case in a classroom. In hockey, there are various ways that players might make themselves crucial to the team's success. There are great goal scorers, great goaltenders and great defensemen, among other things. In a classroom, there are also a variety of ways that students can make themselves important to the "team."

Since I teach social studies, discussion is an important part of my class. A good classroom discussion can do a lot to make seemingly very dry words from a text come alive, and it can obviously make a class a lot more fun. If students don't enjoy the subject they're supposed to be studying or don't care about it, they probably won't gain any lasting learning.

I've attempted to conduct classroom discussions about the same set of questions in different classes on the same day and often gotten vastly different results. In one class, the students may continue an argument as they leave the class, even bringing it into their later classes that day. But in another class, the students seem to be attending a funeral. Same teacher, same topic, same questions, but totally different responses. The difference always depends on just a few students.

Recently I had one student who was particularly good during our class discussions. Nick was a bright, good-natured young man, who knew how to laugh at himself (and others) and loved to argue. He could get himself to really care about things that happened 100 or 200 years ago—not something many high school sophomores do naturally—but when there are one or two students in a class like Nick, class discussions can really take off.

One early December morning that year, our entire high school was shocked to learn that Nick's parents, when they went to wake him up, had found him dead in his bedroom. He had suffered an aneurysm during the night. Obviously, this was a terrible personal tragedy for his family and many friends, and it was also a real blow to our school. His presence was not just missed because of his terrific personality; it was missed because of the contribution he made in every class he attended.

The American history class he was in had been my best discussion class up until the day he died. After that, the class, while okay, wasn't nearly what it had been before. Nick's enthusiasm had been contagious when he was in class, and students who may have started by sitting on their hands were inspired to join the discussion. I can still picture in my mind students who took part in almost every discussion when Nick was there, but almost never got involved after he was gone. For a while, this was likely due to the trauma of his death, but as the year went on, it became clear that it was much more than that. Our discussions in that class were just never able to take off the way they had before, because Nick wasn't there to get his friends going.

Though Nick was unique, many other students have been crucial to the success of different classes for different reasons. For the last few years, I have used cooperative learning in which students work in small groups. I used to be pretty skeptical about this method of teaching, but after learning more about it, experimenting with it, and getting positive feedback from my students, I've come to believe it has some benefits, so I now use it once or twice a week.

A key to making cooperative learning a useful tool rather than a waste of time is putting the right people together in the groups. This is not easy. A couple of years ago, I had one student named Jake, and he was a one-man destruction crew for any group he was in. He was very loud, and early in the year he intimidated all the other members of the groups in which I placed him. His opinions made no sense, because he never read the assignments and never really listened in class. Despite this, he would try to dominate his groups and insult anyone who disagreed with him.

In an effort to get Jake under control, I put him into a group with Matt, who was on the student council and was also one of the better athletes in the school. I thought that if anyone could control Jake, Matt could. I was wrong. Matt was a wonderful athlete, a great student, and a good student council member, but one of the reasons he was elected to the council was that the other kids liked him. He was a very nice young man who was polite to *everybody*, and polite and nice just didn't work with Jake. When they did group work, Jake would bluster and blurt out stupid comments, and Matt would sit there quietly, not really knowing what to say. I knew how he felt!

The experts say that, for cooperative learning to be successful, students need to stay in the same groups for at least a few weeks. But with Jake in the mix, I was making so many changes that I was beginning to feel like George Steinbrenner. Finally, I hit on a winner when I put Jake into a group with Melisa. Melisa was a good student, but not a great one. She would take part in class discussions sometimes, but not always. But when it came to working in groups, and especially in dealing with Jake, she was nothing less than sensational.

When Melisa was put into a small group, she would automatically take charge. She had a competence about her that everyone seemed to sense, and if there was a job to be done, everyone knew she would probably figure out how to do it. She was from a working-class family, as was Jake, and I think this helped her deal with him. I also suspect that he had a mild crush on her, which didn't hurt. In any case, after I put them both into a group, and he would blurt out his nonsense, Melisa would tell him where he was wrong. When he would insult her, she would laugh and insult him right back. Somehow, Melisa was able to get Jake to focus on the group's assignment. Sometimes I would have the groups work together to learn something, and test them with a quiz at the end of the hour. If everyone in the group reached a certain standard, all the students in the group would earn bonus points. Jake was definitely not a fast learner, but Melisa would patiently work with him until he got it, while the other group members worked with each other. That group almost always got the bonus points. Although I use cooperative learning only once or twice a week, it is an important part of my classes, and I would have to say that Melisa saved that class. By taking charge of Jake, she transformed the entire class from one that would have been mediocre at best into one that was pretty good. As a teacher, I'd love to take credit for having accomplished that, and I suppose I deserve some for juggling the lineup until I found that combination, but there is no way I deserve as much as that incredible girl.

I have had students who have clearly made my classes better than they might have been, and I have also had students who have made me a better teacher. If I had to name my all-time favorite student, it would probably be a Laotian girl, Linda, who I had in class about ten years ago. When people think of students participating in class, they usually think of them answering questions, but this girl was exceptional because of the questions she *asked*. Whenever I gave any type of written assignment, Linda was relentless in her questioning, trying to find out exactly what she was supposed to do and making sure she thoroughly understood the material. She was as inquisitive whenever I lectured, and she would ask questions because she was truly interested. If something didn't make sense to her, she wouldn't hesitate to ask for a further explanation in her polite, friendly way.

It's impossible to overstate the value of a student who's willing to ask questions in class. Most students are afraid to ask, because they consistently overestimate the knowledge and understanding of the other kids in the class. That is, they're afraid they might sound stupid. Many students also do a poor job paying attention in class so they're afraid they might be asking a question that has just been asked. Linda never had to worry about that because she always paid attention.

Linda consistently asked those questions that other students were afraid to ask, and she asked them better than anyone else could. She had a way of getting to the point and finding ways to explain to me why she and other students were confused, something that I've never seen in any student before or since. She helped me realize that there were things that I had been teaching for years that a lot of students probably weren't getting. Encouraged by her questions, I would find out that, if I explained just a little further or if I put something just a little differently, that "Oh, I get it!" look would flash across the students' faces. Having Linda in class for a year was as valuable to my teaching as any education class that I've ever had.

Nick, Melisa, and Linda are obvious cases of students who are assets to a school, but most of the kids who are assets are not so obvious. In fact, every student who has a real desire to learn and to do well is an asset to a school. There are the very bright students whose presence and intelligence clearly make their classes better. These kids can finish reading an assignment in about half the time it takes others, and their comprehension is flawless. They ask great questions, and it seems that every time they're called on they have the correct answers. Sometimes they don't raise their hands as often as they could because they don't want to be seen as showing off. When I put them in groups, I know that they will lead their groups and their groups' work will be excellent. When I grade objective tests and find any of their answers wrong, I know I better go back and check the key. I usually find that I'm the one who made a mistake.

There are also students who may not be historical wizards, but who succeed because of their work ethic and persistence. It takes them longer to read assignments than many of the other students, but they get it done. When they answer questions orally in class, they'll be wrong as often as they are right. They'll have to study longer for a test than those really bright students, but they'll put in the work, and if they don't get as high a score, they'll be close.

Then there are the quiet, reliable ones, the students who never raise their hands, but always have their assignments done and are always prepared for tests. Many experts emphasize student participation in class, and I don't deny the importance of that. As a teacher, I certainly want a fair amount of students to raise their hands, ask and answer questions, and participate in other ways, but as I often tell parents jokingly, the more I've taught, the more I've grown to appreciate those quiet kids. They may not say much, but their quiet diligence definitely makes the classes that they are in better.

There is one other type of good student who is the most impressive of all. Over the years I have seen a number of kids who were wonderful students despite living under extremely trying circumstances. This type of student might live in an impoverished trailer and come to school day after day in ragged clothes and with unwashed hair. She might have a mother, father, or both who are the very definition of bad parents. She might have three or four siblings in school who are nothing but trouble. Somehow, however, this young person has managed to rise above her situation. I never know what has enabled this type of student to persevere. Maybe it was a great teacher that she had in elementary school, or maybe it was a wonderful grandparent, or maybe it's just something within her. No student deserves more than she does to be in a class with other good students.

Those great classes that I described at the beginning of the chapter had enough students who were assets in various ways to make them good. They truly were cases of the whole being greater than the sum of its parts. Those good students made each other and everyone else in the class better. If one of those good students had been taken out of his class, it would still have been a good class, though that student would have been missed. If three or four had been taken out, though, the entire personality of the class would have changed. That's all it might have taken— three or four students removed from a class of between twenty-five or thirty, and a great class could have been turned into one that was not much better than average. Same teacher, same school, same classroom, but a very different class.

In essence, most high school students are neither fantastic assets nor terrible disruptions on their own. Most students are essentially what I was, somewhere in the middle; willing to follow the direction of the class in general. If they are in a class with enough good, solid students, they become pretty good students, too. Average students don't like feeling like oddballs, so none of them wants to be the only one who didn't do an assignment, and none of them wants to have the lowest score on a test. But if average students are in a class with a few mildly disruptive kids, they can become real problems themselves. When I was in a class like that, I was the laugher. I wouldn't do anything terribly outrageous myself, but I would laugh the loudest at those who did. Needless to say, the teachers in those classes did not look upon me fondly and, by being the laugher, I sometimes got myself into more trouble than the students who committed the outrageous acts. Now that I've been teaching for thirty years, I've had a few laughers of my own, and I can't say that I blame those teachers who were ready to wring my neck.

Obviously, those "in the middle" kids learn a lot more when they are in a class with other good students than they do when they are in a classroom with the disruptive ones. Since the "in the middle kids" make up the largest group, we should try to increase the chances that they will end up in classes with good students if we want to improve public education. Instead, we have done just the opposite.

This began with court rulings in the 1960s and 1970s that declared public education to be a property right that cannot be taken away without due process of law. Consequent legislation has been passed making it nearly impossible for public schools to remove disruptive students. For example, Minnesota's Pupil Fair Dismissal Act provides for thousands of dollars worth of hearings, lawyers, judges, and appeals before a school can expel a student. Even then, the school is still responsible for finding and paying for an alternate way to provide that student with an education. The message to public schools is clear: unless and until disruptive students bring weapons to school, you are expected to tolerate them. Making matters worse, recent laws and court rulings have encouraged homeschooling and promoted parents using school vouchers to send their kids to private schools. In other words, we are now encouraging good students to leave the public schools. I can't think of a more effective way to destroy public education.

What Makes a Student Good?

In the last chapter, I boasted about the accomplishments of some of my school district's former students. Those of us who have worked in our schools are very proud of them. But, while our school certainly deserves some credit for providing opportunities, most of the credit belongs to those former students themselves. They are the ones who had to make the decision to do the things necessary to take advantage of those opportunities, to work hard and make sacrifices. No one could force those students who excelled in academics to be conscientious about doing their schoolwork. They passed up a lot of things that would have been temporarily fun in order to do as well on their schoolwork as they did. They deserve the credit for taking the path they did, just as they would deserve the blame if they hadn't.

The general public has always seemed to believe that the key to a student's success in school is his academic ability. A student's performance depends, we often think, on whether or not the student is "smart." The A students are "smart," whereas the D students aren't. My experiences as a teacher have convinced me that intellectual ability is not the most important factor. Any teacher or high school student can tell stories about kids with relatively low ability who do amazingly well because they try hard. They can also tell you about kids with a lot of ability who do poorly because they just don't care. There is no question that students with less ability will experience more frustrations and setbacks than will students with greater intellectual ability. They will need more help and encouragement, and most schools bend over backward to provide it. Nevertheless, the major factor in a student's performance is his or her effort. Students who take education seriously and try hard do well. Students who don't care about school do poorly. The single biggest problem in education today is that not enough students in public schools make their own education a very high priority.

For a number of years early in my career, I taught seventh grade classes and twelfth grade classes. Eventually I had twelfth graders who had once been in my seventh grade classes. I can still picture certain students who as seventh graders had a hard time with the material, but who worked very hard, often ending up with C+'s. As seniors, they were much more successful. They still had to work hard, but now they were earning A-'s and B+'s. On the other hand, I can also remember students with so much ability as seventh graders that, with very little effort, they would earn B's and sometimes even A's. By the time these students were seniors, they were down to C's and D's. At some point along the way, their ability ceased to carry them.

Every so often during my teaching career I will have some sort of epiphany and, about twenty years ago, I had a very depressing one. I was correcting a final test I had given, and thinking about the students who were earning C's and D's. At that time, I used sixty percent as the cutoff for passing, and the final test was made up entirely of multiple choice and matching questions. Since a monkey should have been able to get between twenty and twenty-five percent of the test answers correct, it was clear that students earning between sixty and seventy-five percent weren't learning much.

After that final test, I made a major effort to become more creative in my teaching. The students I was most concerned about were those who seemed mired in mediocrity, so they were the targets of most of my new ideas. Some of these ideas created a tremendous amount of work for me and, one day a couple of years later while carrying out one of those ideas, I had another epiphany. I looked out into the classroom and it was clear that many of my C and D students were putting forth their usual effort—little or none. While I was working my backside off, the kids I was trying to help wouldn't lift their fingers to help themselves.

Since that time, I have continued to try to reach as many kids as I can, but I have also geared more and more of my teaching strategies toward encouraging student effort. Students who try hard consistently are probably going to earn pretty good grades in my classes. Students who don't try stand a very good chance of failing.

The lack of effort by kids who fail my classes never ceases to amaze me. There are students who never—and I mean never—attempt to do any of the homework assignments, and there is no guarantee they'll do any work in class, either. There are education critics out there who would be more than happy to assign the blame for the poor performance of these students on public schools and teachers, but what can be done for kids who won't try?

Amazingly, some of these students are honestly surprised when they see the F's on their report cards. Ironically, some of them only try during the last week of a marking period, when their situation is completely hopeless. I always find myself speechless when one of these kids, who may be twenty to thirty percentage points below the passing minimum, comes up to me and asks if he can do extra credit, or asks, "What can I do to pass?" (Be reincarnated!) Since I post grades regularly, students always know where they stand in the class over the course of a marking period, but they think if they give it the old college try for a whopping five days, the teacher will give them a break. I think part of the problem is that too many of these students have already received too many breaks.

Making a Decision

When I was hired in Warroad sixteen years ago, the school district had also hired a new librarian, Dennis Jerome. He and I had both come to Warroad from Minnesota's Iron Range, so we talked frequently, and I found him to be one of the best "common sense" educators I've ever known. One day, he and I were with a group of teachers, when someone mentioned that a student named Debbie had dropped out of school. Dennis immediately said, "Good for her! Debbie finally made a decision."

You might think this was a sarcastic remark, but Dennis was completely sincere. His "Good for her!" expressed as much pride for the girl as would an announcement that she had been accepted into a college. It may seem heretical for anyone in education to praise someone for dropping out of school, but for some students, it is a step forward.

We all would have loved to see Debbie decide to try to be successful as a student, but that wasn't going to happen. For reasons of her own, she had given up long before, and she was simply going through the motions in school. Sometimes she would show up for her classes, but other times she wouldn't, and she would never do work that had been assigned. She had multiple F's on her report cards, so there was no graduation in her foreseeable future. Her horrible grades weren't the result of any learning disability; she just didn't care about her education. Finally, Debbie decided to quit wasting her and everybody else's time, and to get on with her life. Dennis Jerome was absolutely right. Good for her!

Being in school, by itself, has no educational value. Many intelligent people, some of whom make decisions that affect schools, don't seem to understand this. Our county court used to regularly put delinquents on probation, with the condition that they go to school. This might have been a good idea if some standard of performance had been set for these kids, but that was not the case. I would guess the people responsible for setting the probation conditions—the county attorney, the probation officer, and the judge—assumed that, when in school, any student will automatically pay a reasonable amount of attention in class, read at least a few assignments, and do some homework. They were wrong! One student who was forced back into our school would frequently roam the halls during class time and, when asked if he was concerned that this might affect his probation, he answered: "The judge just told me I had to be in school. He didn't say anything about going to class."

Many public officials also don't understand that every student has an effect on other students. When someone is simply "in school," caring nothing about actually getting an education, the effect can only be bad. It is time for that student to make the same decision Debbie did, and if he won't, we should be able to make that decision for him. The last thing we need is to be forced to keep additional disruptive and non-performing students in our schools.

This is not to say that dropouts should never be able to change their minds. Several years ago, *60 Minutes* ran a segment about a program in Chicago in which former dropouts were encouraged to come back to school if they had finally decided that education mattered. The students featured in the story were in their twenties and thirties, and they were all doing well. I don't know if that program is still in existence today, or if it was a success or a failure, but the idea had great merit.

Having twenty-five- and thirty-year-olds roaming around the halls with high-school-aged students is something that would have to be monitored closely. But if it could be assured that those older students were sincere in their newly found desire to get an education, their presence could be very beneficial. I can't imagine a better example to a potential sixteen- or seventeen-year-old dropout than someone who had gone that route, learned through painful experience that it was not a good way to go, and was now showing up regularly for classes, doing homework, reading assignments, and studying for tests. Though I am only speaking for myself when I say this, I think most teachers feel the same way. I don't care how old someone is, what his history is, or how much natural ability he has. If someone really has the desire to get an education, I would love to have him in my class.

Children Left Behind?

Critics are very quick to blame public schools for students who lack motivation. They say public education isn't "reaching" these kids. I remember a talk show I saw on TV a couple of years ago in which the host and a guest representing some educational reform group wrapped up a segment on public education by saying that low test scores weren't the fault of students or their parents. It's everyone else's fault: state legislature's, teachers' union's, school board's, etc. While statements like these may sound good to the public, they are false, and don't help to bring about the "high standards" in public education that this program supposedly promoted.

The popular belief that it's the school's fault if a student isn't performing well became public policy in 2002 when President Bush signed into law the latest program for national educational reform. Both Republicans and Democrats supported this bill, and the very name of the program, No Child Left Behind, makes it hard for me to be open-minded. The clear implication is that low-performing students do poorly because people in those schools have been neglecting them, or, in other words, leaving them behind. And how can we remedy this situation? By identifying "failing schools," with their negligent educators, and punishing them, of course!

There are a number of wealthy suburbs surrounding the Twin Cities area in Minnesota—communities like Edina, Apple Valley, Eden Prairie and Lakeville. The NCLB program is set up in such a way that nearly every public school in America will eventually fall into the "failing" category, but my guess is that these schools will be some of the last ones to do so. On the other hand, I have a sneaking suspicion that some of the inner-city schools of Minneapolis and St. Paul will be designated as failing schools very quickly. When that happens, the NCLB program will encourage us to shake our heads and say, "Boy, all those teachers and principals and everyone else working in those schools must be doing lousy jobs!"

I hope our school in Warroad won't fall into the failing category any time soon, but as should be very clear by now, we do have our share of low-performing students. Our school has tried everything we can think of to help them, and we spend far more money, time, and attention on them than on anyone else. Most of the phone calls we make and letters we send to homes involve these students. So do many of the meetings we attend after school hours. We have special education and individual education plans. We've tried having basic classes, and we've tried mainstreaming. Some of us have tried mastery learning, some of us have tried cooperative learning, and many of us have tried to incorporate other teaching methods into our classes. We believe that some of these changes have made our classes better for all of our students, and some of them have helped to bring along some students who weren't performing well. Nevertheless, we all continue to have some of those low performers who do almost nothing to help themselves. I know that I speak for a lot of other teachers when I say that it's not a matter of our leaving them behind; it's a matter of it being impossible to get them to come along.

Students perform poorly not because schools don't care about them but, in the great majority of cases, because the students don't care themselves. If we really want to improve education in America, we need to start by making it clear that the student, more than anyone else, is responsible for his or her own education. Instead, our society has decided to treat low performing students as victims. If they are victims, then they are victims of poor parenting, the negative influence of bad friends, and their own poor decisions. If there are any victims of the public education system, they are the kids who are stuck with these apathetic and disruptive students in their classrooms.

The Trees From Which
the Apples Fall

While students should be expected to be responsible for their own attitudes, there are many things that influence them, and school is just one of those things. Kids today are strongly influenced by their neighborhoods, their friends, and our culture with its heavy emphasis on entertainment. Many of the movies our kids watch, video games they play, and athletes and rock stars they look up to don't exactly promote positive educational values.

The biggest influence on any student is obviously his or her family, and in most cases, students with parents who place a high priority on education make a reasonable effort and do well. Having great parents doesn't guarantee that kids will be great students—my student career is a testimony to that—but it definitely increases the chances that they will at least be adequate. On the other hand, students with parents who don't make education a priority usually don't try very hard and don't do very well. But let's face it, when that happens, it's a lot easier to say we've got a lot of lousy schools than it would be to say we've got a lot of lousy parents. Well, I'm here to tell you we do have some lousy parents.

Here is an e-mail that was circulating a while ago that many people who work in schools could relate to:

The following is an answering machine message for the Pacific Palisades High School in California. The school and teachers were being sued by parents who wanted their children's failing grades changed to passing grades even though those children were absent fifteen to thirty times during the semester and did not complete enough school work to pass their classes. This was voted unanimously by the office staff as the actual message for the school:

> *"Hello! You have reached the automated answering service of your school. In order to assist you in connecting with the right staff member, please listen to all your options before making a selection:*
>
> *To lie about why your child is absent - Press 1*
>
> *To make excuses for why your child did not do his work - Press 2*
>
> *To complain about what we do - Press 3*
>
> *To swear at staff members - Press 4*
>
> *To ask why you didn't get information that was already enclosed in your newsletter and several flyers mailed to you - Press 5*
>
> *If you want us to raise your child - Press 6*
>
> *If you want to reach out and touch, slap or hit someone - Press 7*
>
> *To request another teacher for the third time this year - Press 8*
>
> *To complain about bus transportation - Press 9*
>
> *To complain about school lunches - Press 0*
>
> *If you realize this is the real world and your child must be accountable/responsible for his/her own behavior, class work, homework, and that it's not the teacher's fault for your children's lack of effort,*
>
> *Hang up and have a nice day!"*

Part of this e-mail was fact, and part of it was fiction. Pacific Palisades High School was being sued, but this message wasn't actually played on the school's answering machine. In fact, the high school didn't even have a menu-based phone system. Nevertheless, I think it's safe to say that it speaks of the frustration that a lot of teachers feel in dealing with some parents.

Don't get me wrong. There are also a lot of very good parents. Twice every year during conferences, I talk with concerned parents who are supportive of both their kids and our school. They want to make sure their kids are behaving well (they almost always are), and they let teachers know they want to be informed right away if there are any problems. The kids of some of these parents are so good that it's hard to find a lot to say. I'll tell the parents that their kids do all their assignments, they always come to class prepared, they do a great job on tests, they participate in class discussions, they're polite, and I love having them in class. The parents will sit, and smile at me, and wait for more. I can't really think of anything more than that to say. Their kids are great students! But who can blame those parents for wanting to hear even more? There is nothing so rewarding as hearing wonderful things about your own children, and the parents who have raised those kids have obviously been doing something very right. They deserve all the praise and admiration they can get.

Although I was not the wonderful student described above, I did have great parents. They emphasized the importance of education, and it was clear from the earliest time I can remember that they expected me to go to college. All the C's I got in high school definitely weren't due to their lack of concern. I never gave them any reason to expect me to be an A student, so they weren't overly pushy, but they would have liked to see me get a lot more B's. I never feared a severe punishment for the C's that I earned, but I felt rotten when I disappointed them with some of my poorer report cards.

Not all of my teachers were great, but the idea of blaming any of them for any of my grades was not something my parents would have considered. I remember them saying negative things about a teacher only once, and that was about one of my brother's teachers. There were times as a student that I might have suffered minor injustices, but I would not have been foolish enough to complain to my parents about it. The teachers and the school were right—period! It was my job to do what my teachers wanted me to do, to the best of my ability. If I did something wrong and got into trouble, I should expect to suffer the consequences, whatever they might be, and make sure I didn't do it again.

There are still parents like that today, but I think it's clear that there were a lot more parents like that when I was going to school. One reason parents have become more difficult for schools to deal with is that the definition of a "good parent" has changed in the minds of many people. They think that instead of supporting teachers and the school, as my parents did, a good parent should make sure the teachers and the school are doing what the parents think they should, and to serve as advocates for their kids whenever the students have conflicts with teachers or principals.

Sol Stern, in *Breaking Free*, certainly seems to have been influenced by this line of thinking. Stern describes being in constant contact with his children's teachers and administrators, and being very willing to challenge their teaching methods. He says that he and his wife, who was also a teacher, gave their children supplementary assignments at home when they felt they weren't being taught correctly. At one point, they even refused to allow one of their children to do an assignment the teacher had given, and gave the child a different assignment in its place.[8] Stern has fond memories of his days in public schools, in the good ol' days of the 1940's and 50's, but one has to wonder if his parents took the same approach that he has taken.

I have to admit, however, that there are times when normally supportive parents should speak up rather than simply say, "Do what the teacher says!" I deal with 150 students in school and forty in hockey, so I'm going to make some mistakes. There have been times when parents have pointed out that I've done something as simple as recording the wrong test score for a student. There have been times when parents have given me information to make me realize that I needed to change my approach to a student. There have been times when parents have politely told me that they disagreed with something I have done while acknowledging that they understood my reasons. And there have also been times when I've had to look a parent in the eye and say, "You're right; I screwed up! Now what can we do to correct it?"

The key is for parents to approach these situations with the presumption that the teacher or teachers involved are competent and want to do the right thing. Many parents don't do this. Instead, they immediately assume that the teacher or the principal or whoever else from the school who is involved is wrong or lazy or acting out of ulterior motives. Obvi-

8. Stern, *Breaking free*, 61

ously, the media's constant barrage of criticism of public education helps fuel this assumption. With all the talk about "failing schools," and with talking heads like Brit Hume constantly reporting stories about how schools have messed up, it is no wonder that many parents aren't willing to give schools and teachers the benefit of the doubt.

Another reason that so many parents are confrontational in their relationship with schools is that some of them simply want to be their children's friends, and they naively believe whatever their children tell them. I can recall a conference I had with a single mother a few years ago that serves as a perfect example. This woman's daughter was a bright girl who squeaked by in the first marking period with a C-. She was capable of much better work than this, and sometime during the middle of the quarter I sent a deficiency report home to the mother, detailing the things that the girl wasn't doing.

When the mother showed up for her conference, I began by saying what a bright girl I thought her daughter was, and that she was really capable of earning A's and B's in American History. When I began to explain why I thought she was so capable, and to tell the mother the simple things her daughter could do to bring up her grade, she said to me, "Well, you know, the kids say you favor the athletes."

It quickly became apparent that the mother had already determined that I was guilty as charged. After all, I'm a coach, and everyone knows that the only thing coaches really care about is sports. When the deficiency report had gone home, the daughter's defense had been that I "favored the athletes," and a girlfriend who was failing the class, and who would end up dropping out had backed her up. It made no difference to the mother that I had also sent deficiency reports to more football players, and put more of them on our scholastic ineligibility list, than any other teacher in the high school that fall. Her daughter had told her that I favored the athletes, and her daughter's friend had agreed. So it must be true.

That mother had come into our conference, not with a presumption that the teacher was incompetent, but with a presumption that the teacher was unfair. The point of the conference to that mother was not to find out what her daughter could do to learn more and earn a better grade, but to let me know that she was onto me. She knew I was unfair, and that's why I had sent her the deficiency report, and that's why her daughter's grade wasn't higher. I was the one who would have to change.

That might have been reasonable if I had been unable to show the mother all the evidence of the assignments that her daughter had failed to turn in, and all the classes that she had missed for frivolous reasons, with excuses signed by the mother herself. It would have been different if there had been some pattern of athletes earning higher grades than they deserved in my class, or being given other kinds of favors, but there were no such patterns.

That conference was a complete waste of time and effort. The one person who had the power to change something to bring about more learning and a better grade—the daughter—now would have absolutely no incentive to improve. What is really distressing is that the mother probably went away from that conference feeling very good about herself as a parent. She had stood up for her daughter! She had told off that nasty old teacher! She had been her daughter's advocate!

There are other parents like that mother, and their children are usually less than a pleasure to work with. For nine years I ran the Little League baseball program in Warroad. We had a very low-key house league, and I served as league director, co-coach of the teams, and umpire for the games. I remember one time when I was working as a base umpire; I could hear two mothers sitting in lawn chairs chatting about their dealings with our middle school teachers and principal. They were both trying to one-up the other with stories about the brave stands they had taken. It was, "I told him" this, and "I let him know" that, and "they better not try" this, and "I'm not going to put up with" that. The bottom line was that they did not want anyone in the middle school doing anything to discipline their kids.

I might have entertained the possibility that our middle school was doing something wrong if I hadn't seen those kids in action in baseball day after day during the summer. We had very few discipline problems in our league, but those two were troublemakers. They were constantly loud, obnoxious, and arguing with someone. A few years later, when they entered our high school, they were both constantly in trouble, until they were finally sent to our alternative learning center. Neither of them ended up graduating, but I would bet anything that to this day neither of those parents sees anything wrong with the approach they took in dealing with their kids or the school.

Some parents like this become downright belligerent. A few years ago, one father came into the school for a meeting with me in the spring, just a few weeks before the end of the year. His son had failed all three marking periods, and was well on his way to making it four for four. He was also one of the most disruptive students I've ever had in class, but he had managed to remain there despite my constant lobbying to the principal to have him removed.

From the time he walked into my room, this father was full of tough-guy talk. He said over and over that his son's whole year had been a waste, and it was my fault. His most important, specific complaint was that I should have allowed him into my basic class. I explained to him that our basic class worked well because we reserved it for students who had difficulty in social studies despite making a good effort, and we feared that we would ruin the class if we allowed disruptive students in it. Not surprisingly, my explanation didn't satisfy him.

Then he started to chew me out because I should have told him and his wife how badly things were going, so they could send their son to the alternative learning center. When I pulled out a letter that I had sent to them early in the year recommending just that, he blamed the school secretaries for never sending it. When it became clear that the secretaries had sent it, he blamed the post office for losing the letter. It apparently never occurred to him that his fine son, whose year had been wasted, might have intercepted it.

This guy looked like he'd had a few barroom brawls, and he probably thought he was going to physically intimidate me. Actually, this was really a dangerous situation because, rather than being intimidated, I became furious. For eight months, I had had to put up with this guy's offspring. The kid never had anything good to say about anyone, and whoever he disagreed with was either "gay," "a homo," or " a queer." He was continually obnoxious, and he definitely made it harder for me to do my job, and harder for the other students in his class to learn. By the time dear old Dad came in, I had sent home eight letters reporting on his son's lack of progress, and there had been two conferences at school. I never heard one word from him until he decided to come in and give me a piece of his mind, less than one month before the end of the school year.

Mercifully, most parents are not that way. I've had less than a handful of parents like the tough-talking father, and for every mother like the one who was so willing to believe her daughter's excuses, I've had several who either didn't buy excuses at all, or waited until they heard the teacher's side of the story to come to a decision. I don't know how many times I've heard parents say, "Ah, I thought there was more to it than what he was saying!"

On the whole, most parents are actually pretty good, and most of their kids are pretty good additions to class. Every so often, a blatantly disruptive or apathetic student will come from a family with parents who seem to be concerned and reasonable people, and I can only feel sympathy for them. But usually, when I have students like that, I find that the apple hasn't fallen very far from the tree. Schools try to turn students like that around, and every so often a miracle results. We cannot be expected to do that consistently, however. Yet, it often seems that politicians, the media, and the general public think we should be able to do just this.

Many of us who work in public education might fall over in a faint if our critics ever showed that they recognized how important parenting is to the effectiveness of schools. Our society needs to understand that, no matter how good a school is, it needs competent parents as partners in order to give a child the best chance to get the education he or she deserves. Without good, supportive parents, the school will be fighting an uphill battle.

Did You Know We Fought China in the Revolutionary War?

I am so tired of hearing stories about "man on the street" surveys in which high school students or graduates or even college students fail to answer simple questions.

Question: Who did America fight in the Revolutionary War?

Answers: Japan, China, the Soviet Union, or even Vietnam or Korea.

Question: Who was the president during the Civil War?

Answers: Ronald Reagan, Richard Nixon, or maybe Benjamin Franklin.

Naturally, the sad results of these surveys imply that our public schools are doing a lousy job of teaching American history. All I can tell you is that, when my class finishes a unit on the Revolutionary War, students earning passing grades know that we fought Great Britain. When we finish our unit on the Civil War, they know that Abraham Lincoln was president. They also remember the answers to those questions at the end of the first semester and at the end of the year. I have some control over what my students know when I have them in class, but I can't control what they are going to know several years later. We have quizzes on these things, we have multiple choice tests on these things, and we have essay tests which include questions about these things. I have the students read about them, we have group and class discussions about them, and I do the best I can to make it interesting when I talk about them. But if students don't care about American history and related issues, and if they receive no reinforcement in their homes or in any other areas of their lives, then there's a good chance that, if you ask them those very simple questions a couple of years after they've taken my class, they'll give the same stupid answers we've heard people give for the last several years.

If anyone had asked me those questions when I was in third or fourth grade, I would have been able to answer them correctly, and it's not because my school did a better job teaching me. I might have learned the answers there first, but they got reinforced because social issues mattered in my home. My parents were lower-middle-class people, but we always had news magazines and newspapers in our home, and Walter Cronkite or Chet Huntley and David Brinkley were regular dinner guests. My parents didn't talk only about politics and history, but those things were included in their conversation at least once in a while.

This is not the case for many of the students I've been teaching for the last thirty-one years. Every year I ask the students in my classes how many of them watch news programs, and I can't remember the last time I've seen more than two hands. In most of the classes, there are none. The students don't know the name of the vice president, they don't know who their senators or representatives are, and they've never known any of our state officials except for our previous governor, Jesse "The Body" Ventura.

Today there are many tools that can be used to reinforce the things teachers teach in social studies classes. There are the cable TV news networks, there is the History Channel, and A&E has some excellent programs. Kids can also use the Internet to keep up with what's going on in the world and to learn about past events or people. Some of my students do take advantage of these resources, and you can bet that they aren't going to be the ones who think we fought China in the Revolutionary War.

It would be a wonderful world for social studies teachers if those were the only things in the media for students to explore, but they're not. In addition to the news networks, we have ESPN and ESPN2. As alternatives to the History Channel and A&E, there are HBO, Showtime, Cinemax, VH1, and MTV. If a typical 16-year-old male is channel surfing and has to pick between a documentary on the Battle of the Bulge and a music video featuring the hottest new female star writhing around in an outfit that leaves almost nothing to the imagination, which one do you think he'll pick? And the Internet provides much more than just information on current events or history. And, hey, if for some reason the Internet has gone on the blink, you can always play a video game, go get a DVD, or listen to a little gangsta rap on a CD.

There was a time in our history when the heroes of our society were businessmen like Andrew Carnegie and John D. Rockefeller. When I was growing up, a lot of kids, rightly or wrongly, looked at John F. Kennedy as a role model. If you asked kids who they view as role models today, given all of the emphasis in our culture on entertainment, celebrities and immediate gratification, who do you think more would pick: Peyton Manning or George W. Bush? Faith Hill or Hillary Clinton? Snoop Dogg or Colin Powell?

While we now have at our fingertips more information about the past and the present than we've ever had before, we also have the opportunity to ignore more. Many young people, with the acquiescence of their parents, are choosing to do just that.

There are some young people today who come from families in which politics and social issues are important, and they stick out in their classes like Jesse Ventura in a Harvard political science class. However, most of the students we teach in social studies are getting almost no reinforcement in other areas of their lives. As a result, it becomes very difficult to get them to care about history, current events, or social issues of any kind. So the next time you see someone in a "man on the street" interview come off like an idiot because he can't answer a simple question, one with an answer he should have learned in school, don't assume that it's the school's fault. It's entirely possible he simply chose to be ignorant.

Thirty Hours, My Foot!

In *Breaking Free,* Sol Stern describes "by the rules" teachers who work a maximum of thirty hours per week in the New York City public schools, and make $81,000 doing it.[9] I don't know how many teachers in New York City fit that description, but I do know people would be wrong to assume that's generally the case for teachers across the country.

I generally spend between fifty and sixty hours each week working directly on my teaching duties. On most days, I arrive at school between 6:45 and 7:00 AM, and I go home at about 3:45 PM. I will frequently either bring papers to correct home with me, or go back to the school for about an hour at night, and I spend several hours there every weekend. Like many other teachers, I also coach and, when I'm doing that, my workweek gets significantly longer.

Our classes run from 8:19 AM until 3:00 PM, with twenty-six minutes for lunch, which I eat in my room while working, and a forty-nine minute preparation period. Besides running my six classes each day, I spend time preparing upcoming units, revising curriculum, making copies, correcting the endless flow of papers and make-up work, monitoring hallways, averaging grades, preparing deficiency slips, and putting together weekly lists of students who are failing.

9. Stern, *Breaking free,* 116

In addition to this, I spend a lot of my spare time on my job. In fact, if you asked me about my hobbies, I'd have to say that my favorite hobby is my job. Ever since my early teaching years, I've enjoyed tinkering with curriculum, coming up with new questions for my classes to debate, and finding different ways to present materials. I've designed my share of miserable failures, but it's a great feeling when I come up with something that really works.

Besides working on curriculum, grading papers, and doing other paperwork, I try to read a few nonfiction books that are relevant to my teaching every year, usually in American history. If I read an 800-page book on Theodore Roosevelt, I might get about fifteen minutes of stories that I can use to make my classes a little more interesting, and it gives me great background. When it comes to reading, I am a plodder, but, hey, I'm fifty-four! If I amble through just a few books every year, after thirty-one years I'll have quite a few stories.

I don't know how many teachers spend more time at their jobs than I do, and I don't know how many spend less, but I can assure you that the amount of time the teachers I know spend at their jobs is a lot closer to what I do than the thirty hours that Stern talks about. And while there may be teachers who earn $81,000 in New York City, I can assure you that no teacher in northern Minnesota is bringing home that kind of money.

Teachers are motivated to spend a great deal of time on their jobs by their love of teaching, but there is also a more practical reason. Teaching is enjoyable for those who come to school prepared and on top of things, but for a person who is unprepared, it is anything but enjoyable. When you're disorganized and have nothing constructive for a class to do, being in charge of twenty-five to thirty adolescents for forty-nine minutes is a nightmare. The kids see through teachers who do that in about two minutes, and it becomes impossible for such teachers to maintain any discipline. A classroom full of bored teenagers is not the place for an unprepared teacher to find mercy. I found myself in that type of situation a few times early in my career, and it didn't take long to figure out that I'd be a lot happier person if I took the time to prepare.

As a teacher, having one bad class in which you are poorly prepared and the kids are out of control is a humiliating experience, and it ruins your day no matter how well the other classes go. To go through that class after class, day after day, would be a living nightmare. I'm sure that being incompetent at any job is unpleasant, but there are few jobs that could be worse to do incompetently than teaching—maybe professional boxing. When Sol Stern talks about all those thirty-hour-per-week teachers, I have trouble believing that there are that many gluttons for punishment. Yes, there are bad teachers, and there are lazy teachers, but I can honestly say that I haven't known very many of them up here in northern Minnesota.

I can only understand a teacher not wanting to be well prepared when being prepared doesn't make any difference. Maybe that's the case in some schools. Lessons that a teacher designs are much more likely to work when there are motivated kids who will give learning a chance, and there have always been plenty of those in the schools in which I've taught. If I were teaching in a situation where there were a lot of disruptions, or the students acted bored no matter what I did, it would be hard to keep putting in the hours that I do.

When I discuss the amount of work that many teachers put into their jobs, I want to address the criticisms of Sol Stern and others, but I'm not looking for praise or sympathy. I know very well that if I want to start complaining about long hours or stress or anything else, I would face those three magical words: THREE MONTHS OFF!

I am fully aware of how much the public resents our having summers off, in part because I happen to be married to a non-teacher. Every time my wife thinks of a home-improvement project that could be done from the beginning of April until September, she will finish by saying, "After all, you have three months off." In fact, the rallying cry of "You have three months off!" is heard more often in our household during the spring and summer than "Remember the Alamo!" was heard during the Texas War for Independence.

As a teacher, all I can say about that is that I didn't make the rules, and I have never seen any indication that the public doesn't want it that way. Parents and other adults might not like seeing teachers having June, July, and August free, but they do want that for their children. Parents want the time so they can take the family on vacation without the kids missing school, and they want their teenagers to have summer jobs. In fact, in 2005 the Minnesota state legislature made it a law that schools can't begin classes before Labor Day. I'm not going to complain about that, and I have to admit that I feel pretty good when June rolls around every year. Nevertheless, getting three months off in the summer was not the reason I went into teaching. So if you're one of those people who want kids to have those three summer months off, please don't be too angry with teachers for having them off as well.

Ways to Skin a Cat

When the media discusses public education, there's a good chance that it will refer to incompetent teachers. We hear a lot about them, but we don't hear enough about teachers like Rafe Esquith who teaches in a large urban school district in California. This amazing fifth and sixth grade teacher has his students come to school two hours early and stay late so that he can spend extra time with them reading or teaching them Shakespeare. He spends his Saturdays helping former students prepare for the SAT, and during his students' recess, he gives them the option of staying in his room where he will teach them to play the guitar. He has made all sorts of sacrifices in order to provide his students with materials and to reward them for good work, such as taking them on trips, or hosting parties for them at his house. Although he is married, he seems to have dedicated almost all of his life to his students. If he is not a candidate for canonization, his wife certainly should be.

Esquith should serve as an inspiration to all teachers, but I'm reluctant to suggest that any of us try to copy him too closely for fear that I'd encourage an epidemic of nervous breakdowns. It is also possible to be a good teacher without doing all the things he does. When it comes to teaching I've learned that there is definitely more than one way to skin a cat. We don't have any Rafe Esquith's in our school, but we've got a lot of good teachers who do different things in different ways.

John Bono is a twenty-eight year veteran who teaches social studies. If I were going to describe him in a short phrase, I would call him a hard-working entertainer. The core of Bono's approach to teaching is his belief that every student should have the opportunity to be successful. He argues that any student, by making a consistent effort, should be able to earn an A or a B. He gives some demanding assignments, but he encourages effort by also designing many short, very doable ones, and making the students accountable for all of them. Any teacher knows that students are notorious for not doing reading assignments. In order to deal with that problem, Bono wrote his own textbook. His reading assignments are shorter than those in standard textbooks, but because there is no wasted material, and because students know they will be held accountable, they actually read them. Many kids give Bono credit for having done more than any other teacher to help them learn how to become good students.

Bono's most outstanding characteristic, however, is his ability to use self-deprecating humor. Learning this has probably been an absolute necessity, because he tends to be an absent-minded klutz, and he is capable of major bouts of cerebral flatulence. A couple of years ago, he was walking around his classroom checking students' assignments when he heard words from a student that no teacher ever wants to hear: "Mr. Bono, your fly's open."

Bono is probably most famous with students for a lesson he once gave on the Middle East. He had a map on his overhead projector when a fly landed on it, and he decided to smash the bug. Since overhead projectors are made of glass, it wasn't a good idea. The glass plate shattered, of course, but the light stayed on. Up on the screen was Israel with a squashed bug in the middle of it, and lines from the shattered glass extending out in every direction. When explaining the incident to our principal, Bono said that he was teaching the concept of collateral damage.

Although my own style resembles Bono's, the teachers I admire the most are those who take the tough, no-nonsense approach where the teacher is truly the commander of his (or her) classroom. Cary Eades is one of the most successful high school hockey coaches in the history of Minnesota. He guided his teams to one third place finish, two second place finishes, and three state championships during his eleven-year tenure at Warroad. He also trained the coaching staff and most of the players who won another state championship the year after he left. Cary taught weight training classes, and he is a master of the no-nonsense style. I worked with him as his assistant coach, and he exuded toughness and was intimidating without trying to be. He is six-foot-two and about 230 pounds, with dark hair, a dark mustache, and dark eyes: I frequently referred to him as the Latin American Dictator. Put a military hat on him, and he fits the bill perfectly. Fidel Castro, eat your heart out!

The end of Cary's hockey playing career says volumes about this man. After an outstanding college career, he had an opportunity to go straight to the NHL to play with the Minnesota North Stars, who were looking for someone to play the role of enforcer on their team. (For those of you unfamiliar with hockey lingo, an enforcer is someone who goes out and beats up players from the other team.) Cary chose to go to the St. Louis Blues organization instead, because they seemed more interested in him as an all-around hockey player. That meant, however, that he would have to start on one of their minor league teams and wait to be called up. In his second year as a pro, when a call-up to the Blues and the NHL seemed imminent, Cary was skating around the back of his own net in the second period of a game when he ran head first into an opposing player he never saw coming. His neck hurt, but he finished the game. The next day his team had another game, and he played the first two periods before finally telling his coach that his neck was too sore for him to go on. He was sent to a hospital for x-rays, which showed that he had broken and dislocated his neck. The incredibly strong muscles in his neck which had been built up by vigorous weight training saved him from being paralyzed, but his hockey-playing career was over.

I don't know about you, but a stiff neck, even one from having slept the wrong way, can ruin my day. I won't even attempt to play *golf* with it. After suffering a broken and dislocated neck, this man had played in two *professional hockey games*, with two hundred pound bruisers skating around at dizzying speeds, delighting at the opportunity to staple any player from the opposition into the end boards. Cary Eades is a tough guy.

When Cary talks to players on a team or students in a classroom, the kids better have their eyes on him and they better look alert. Most teachers can only envy the attention he gets. Knowing that young people sit in classes for six or seven hours a day, most of us understand that their minds wander from time to time. But not Cary. He is incredibly intense, and students or players quickly see when he is unhappy with the effort they are making. He can scare the devil out of people by talking softly, but he isn't afraid to yell. During his years in Warroad, even I would slink down to the other end of the bench looking for a way to become invisible when a player who made a poor effort or a referee who blew a call had raised the wrath of Eades.

As is often the case with these "tough guy" teachers, Cary would do anything for former players and students who had done their jobs well for him. And I'm not just talking about leading scorers or top weightlifters; I'm also talking about third or fourth-liners, student managers, statisticians, and ninety-eight-pound weaklings—anyone who had worked hard and done his or her best under his watch. In return, Cary and other teachers like him gain the admiration and respect from kids in a way that none of the rest of us can. They are the teachers who most frequently become the role models whom young people try to emulate for the rest of their lives.

This style can be effective in situations other than coaching and physical education classes. Brian Sage was the Government teacher in our school for over thirty years, and he was very much like Cary. Although Brian wasn't close to Cary's size, he was not a guy you'd want to cross. He exuded a wiry intensity, and if you punched him on the shoulder, your hand would hurt for about two days. Every student in the school knew that when they entered his classroom, even if it was just a study hall, they'd better be prepared to work. He commanded the same respect-awe-fear from his students that Cary did and as a result, his students performed extremely well. In an elective class that I taught every year, I would always have some kids who were also taking one of Brian's Government classes. If we ended up giving a test on the same day, I had to face the fact that students weren't going to study for my test first.

All of the teachers I have known who have been masters of this sort of style have been men, but I have heard of women who have taught that way very effectively. The style does seem more natural for men, and I think that has something to do with physical respect. Let's be honest. We're talking about respect, but we're also talking about fear, and that little voice inside a potentially disruptive student that says, "If I'm not careful, that guy just might beat me up!" Obviously, that's not going to happen—not in this day and age, when a teacher might get sued for just hurting a kid's self-esteem. That doesn't stop the idea from occurring to some kids, however, and maybe that's not such a bad thing.

Many people who believe there is not enough discipline in our schools probably believe that every teacher should try to be like Eades and Sage, but it isn't a style for everyone. As much as I admire it, I know it isn't for me, and it certainly isn't for someone like John Bono. Acting like a tough guy when you're prone to doing things like walking around class with your fly open just won't work.

There are other teachers in our school who have different styles because they have different gifts. Deanna Comstock is an English teacher who has a remarkable ability to relate to the students. She has a personality that causes students to like and trust her immediately, and to sense that she really cares about them. She is able to conduct great class discussions about almost anything in almost any type of situation, including study hall! I've seen teachers with that kind of personality who are ineffective because they allow kids to walk all over them, but Deanna happens to combine that personality with common sense. Anyone who thinks he's going to fake her out with a sob story about why he didn't get his assignment done will end up disappointed.

The teachers who probably get the least amount of credit, and yet who amaze me the most, are shop teachers who somehow manage to run productive classes. It's no secret that many of the kids who take shop classes are not the students that other teachers look forward to having in class. They are the ones who cause frequent headaches for teachers like me. You might think that these students would behave a lot better in their shop classes than they do in their academic classes, because the subject matter should be more interesting to them. As someone who has been called on to substitute in those classes from time to time, I can tell you to think again. Although a lack of interest in the subject matter may partially explain their poor performance in academics, lack of self-discipline is often at least as important a factor. There are some kids who really want to learn about carpentry or small engines or welding, but there are many others who are just as ready to misbehave in a shop class as they are in English. The good news is that, in a shop class, they will now be doing hands-on activities, which is a much more effective way of learning for many of them. The bad news is that they will often be working with very dangerous tools and machinery. Imagine being in charge of a bunch of sixteen and seventeen-year olds who are considered "screw-offs," and who are now armed with power saws, welding torches, and nail guns.

One of the shop teachers in our school is a Canadian named Jeremy Culleton, and he somehow manages to develop a great relationship with these kids, while getting them to perform. Jeremy is a self-described former hell-raiser, and he is able to connect with these kids in a way that a teacher like me can only marvel at. In *The Worm in the Apple*, Peter Brimelow ridicules teachers because their average SAT scores weren't as high as college students who went into other professions.[10] I doubt that Culleton's college test scores were off the charts, but I also doubt that there are many SAT wiz-kids who could come close to doing what he does with his students.

I can imagine Brimelow replying that a low-scoring teacher is fine in shop classes, but not in academics. I certainly fit the mold of the teacher whose college test scores were less than impressive, but I don't see this as a disadvantage. The average high school student is, well, average, and I can identify with that student. I remember what it was like not to feel like doing my homework, or to look for shortcuts so I could just get my C. So now, as a teacher, I am constantly looking for ways to get that student to do better, and sometimes I actually succeed because I understand him. Could someone who earned straight A's in high school and throughout college do the same? I don't think so. I am not at all convinced that people who had the highest grades in high school and college and had the highest scores on SAT's or ACT's would always make the best teachers.

On the other hand, there are also teachers like Nola Brandt, who teaches computer classes in our high school, but also doubles as our school district's high tech coordinator. I don't know Nola's ACT score, but I'm pretty sure she beat me. The woman is smart! I have two sons who are making very nice livings due in large part to the start they got in Nola's computer classes. As soon as you talk to her, you know that she was born to be a teacher. She has such a kind, patient manner, and she

10. Brimelow, *The worm in the apple*, 49

explains absolutely everything, whether it's in a workshop that she runs for other teachers, in the classroom with a group of students, or in a two-minute conversation with someone in the hall. When she comes to my room to teach me something new on my computer, she knows that she has to avoid using big words, and sometimes I even understand her.

I realize that my descriptions of six teachers probably won't convince many skeptics that most teachers are as good as I believe they are, especially when critics like Sol Stern and Peter Brimelow imply that there are so many incompetent teachers that you can't help tripping over them if you enter a public school. I have to admit that I have known incompetent teachers. These were teachers who quit making any yearly changes in their curriculum, and they quit preparing for their classes on a day-to-day basis, and they just quit caring. Despite the fact that I completely disagree with our critics about the number of incompetent teachers, I completely agree with them that it should be much easier to get rid of them than it is. Bad teachers give the rest of us a bad name that we don't deserve.

While I can't deny that incompetent teachers exist, I can say that I have known very few of them during my thirty-one year career. In fact, I can count the number of incompetent teachers I've known on the fingers of one hand, while I can't even begin to count the number of teachers I've known who resemble the six teachers I've described above. They've taught my children, I've worked with them in the schools in which I've taught, and I've dealt with them in workshops and coaches clinics I've attended around the state. If my experience in Minnesota is representative at all—and I believe it is—most public school teachers are thoroughly competent, and incompetent teachers are the exception, not the rule.

Of the six teachers I described, only two of them had the same style, yet all of them are effective. That's one thing I'm not sure some educational reformers, especially those who want all teachers to teach the same way, understand. One group of reformers believes that everyone should use cooperative learning. Another group will tell us that we should all have our students working on hands-on projects. Another group will say we should all use mastery learning. Another group will say that we should all fully incorporate multiple intelligences into our classes, and still another group says that we should all get back to basics.

All of those suggestions have some benefits, but no one will be served well if we all turn into teacher-robots. Different teachers doing different things in different ways keeps a school healthy because each student is different. There might be a student who responds to the style of Eades and Sage better than he does to any other teachers. But there might be another student who doesn't respond so well to that style, but is inspired by a teacher like Deanna Comstock. And there may be still others who respond best to the styles of Culleton or Brandt. In our school, as in so many other schools throughout the nation, if a student can't find at least one teacher to inspire him, he probably doesn't want to be inspired.

Tenure, Seniority, and Unions

Many other teachers would say many of the things I say in this book, but now I'm going to say something that I know puts me into a minority: I believe that our tenure and seniority systems, as they are now practiced, are doing more harm than good for teachers and public education.

What I dislike most about the tenure system is that it makes it too difficult to get rid of those few incompetent teachers who give the rest of us a black eye. What I dislike most about the seniority system is its strict last-hired, first-fired rule. I am now in a position where I benefit from it, but that was not the case for most of my career. When I taught in Mt. Iron, I was always a very low man on the seniority totem pole. During the last five to ten years of my tenure, I was one of the hardest-working and most popular teachers on the staff, but this meant nothing when it came to job security. It didn't matter how much time I spent at my job, or how much time I spent trying to get better, or how effective I was in class. It didn't matter that there was another teacher in my field who spent the entirety of his two prep hours smoking cigarettes and drinking coffee in the teachers' lounge. He was higher than I was on the seniority list. Consequently, if cuts had to be made, he would stay and I would go.

When I criticize the seniority system, I am not saying that experience is meaningless. For many of us, including me, it means a lot. I know that I have become a much better teacher with time. If a teacher wants to improve, the things he learns by experience has to help him. He is placed in more and more situations. There are some that he handles well, and some he handles poorly, and he can learn from all of them. Over time, he can also learn more and more about the subjects he teaches, and can continually improve his curriculum. Experience does matter.

But it isn't the only thing that matters, and it doesn't always make a teacher better. There have been a number of times when I've seen a new teacher come into a school, and become one of the most valuable members of its staff in just a couple of years. She might clearly be more of an asset to that school than are some of the older teachers. Perhaps this is because the younger teacher works so hard or is exceptionally talented, but part of it might also be that some of the teachers with seniority feel so safe that they no longer see any need to improve. Although senior teachers rarely become incompetent, I have seen some of them fail to work up to their potential.

There is no question that the results of the seniority system for the schools in which I've taught have been educationally disastrous. In the twelve months before I left Mt. Iron, we lost three of our very best teachers because of the seniority system: Lyle Giersdorf, an outstanding social studies teacher; Kyle Thorson, our best health-physical education teacher; and John Renzaglia, who was one of our best English teachers. Giersdorf and Thorson each coached two sports, and Renzaglia was in charge of speech and drama. None of their contributions mattered, however, when the staff cuts were made.

During my first several years in Warroad, we were in the enviable position of having increasing enrollment, so no cuts were necessary, but lately, that situation has changed. Recently, we lost an excellent young English teacher to another district because her position was so unstable in Warroad, and shortly before I began writing this book, we cut Daryl Frisbie, who is one of the best social studies teachers I've ever known.

Frisbie, who had been a casualty of the seniority system in his previous school, taught civics to ninth-graders. This meant he would have them the year before I got them as sophomores in American history. During the course of the year, I always ask a number of civics-related questions that have to do with the American history topics we are studying. Normally, when students are asked questions, the answers to which they were supposed to learn the year before, a few hands will go up from students who clearly remember the answers, some other students will remember the answers after they hear them, and the remainder will be clueless. When I first began getting students who had Frisbie the year before, nearly every hand in the class would go up when I asked those questions. And he didn't just teach students; he inspired them. There wasn't a week that went by that students in my classes didn't bring up something that Mr. Frisbie had done or told them. It didn't take long before it became obvious that we had picked up a very special teacher.

Nevertheless, when cuts had to be made, our administrators had no choice but to begin shuffling teachers all over the place, putting many into classes they'd never taught before, in order to protect the seniority system. Since Daryl was the low man, he was the one who ended up being cut. You would think a teacher as good as this would have no trouble finding another job, but the hiring system in education isn't much better than the firing system, especially when it comes to social studies. Many school districts have very tight budgets, and they're interested in the bottom line, so they look to spend as little money as possible when hiring new teachers. Their least expensive route is to hire someone just out of college, and if you have a few years of experience, or if you have a Masters Degree, finding another job isn't going to be easy. Frisbie was unable to find another job in Minnesota, so in order to keep teaching, he ended up moving to Alaska. As a result, Warroad High School lost an outstanding teacher and a two-sport coach, along with his wife, who was the cheerleading advisor. Warroad's loss was Alaska's gain.

Defenders of the seniority system argue that without it, teacher cuts would be left up to the principal and the administration, and politics would rear its ugly head. They don't want to see longtime teachers laid off because they've dared to question some administration policy or because they have personality conflicts with a principal. These are valid concerns. I have to admit that there is no perfect system to determine which teachers stay and which teachers go, but I believe we have to do better than one in which the first people to be cut are teachers like Giersdorf, Thorson, Renzaglia and Frisbie.

What I've written over the last few pages may seem like an attack on experienced teachers, but I really don't mean to offer that. Yes, I do think the seniority system results in the loss of excellent teachers, while others who are not as good continue to work. Yes, I think the average teacher would be more highly motivated if there were no such things as the seniority system and tenure. Believe me, however, that doesn't mean that I think that most teachers don't work hard. It also doesn't mean that I think we have a bunch of poor teachers running our schools.

Critics of public school teachers give the impression that if there were no tenure, large numbers of teachers would be replaced. I don't think that would happen, because I believe most of us work hard and do a good job, and I believe most people in our local communities—including our principals—recognize that. I find it interesting that some of the strongest advocates for getting rid of teacher tenure have been disappointed when they have gotten their way. Peter Brimelow bemoans the fact that, after Oregon got rid of teacher tenure, almost every teacher in the state was rehired anyway. He quotes a state senator as saying, "We give them a tool to be able to get some of the poor teachers out of the system, and they just don't use it."[11] It seems never to have occurred to either Brimelow or that state senator that maybe there weren't as many bad teachers as they thought. It seems never to have occurred to many good teachers that maybe the tenure and seniority systems aren't as important to their security as they think.

No aspect of public education has been the brunt of more criticism than teachers' unions, and they have been the strongest defenders of tenure and seniority. I obviously disagree with them on this issue, and I am also uncomfortable with stands they have taken on a number of other issues. I am slightly left of center in my political leanings, but I am not nearly as liberal as they are. Nevertheless, I am not about to attack teachers' unions, because I am very grateful to them.

When I began teaching, my salary was so low that my wife and I qualified for a welfare program. I ate peanut butter and jelly sandwiches for lunch and dinner for an entire month, and my mother-in-law cried during her 200-mile trip home to the Twin Cities after seeing the house we lived in. Furthermore, prior to intervention by the unions, female teachers had been required to leave the classroom as soon as they became pregnant. Things have changed, largely due to the efforts of our teachers'

11. Brimelow, *The worm in the apple,* 221

unions that some critics seem eager to compare to terrorist organizations or the communist party.

At this time, I earn a little more than $50,000 a year for teaching, and a little more than $5,000 for coaching hockey. I know there are people who think that this is too much for a teacher-coach, but I am not going to apologize. When my income is combined with my wife's, we are able to have a very comfortable life, but we're not exactly basking in luxury. That becomes clear to me every time I step into my hail-dented, 1995 Ford Escort to go for a spin. Teaching is an important occupation; I think most people would agree with that. I know how much of teachers' lives and energies go into their jobs, and I don't think there are too many people who surpass us in that area. Despite that, most people with similar education and experience make more money than teachers do, including two of my sons who began making more than me as soon as they stepped out of college. I'm very proud of them for that, but my point is that teachers earn their money. And I have very little doubt that if it weren't for our unions, all teachers would be making a heck of a lot less than we are.

Headaches

"Education is one of the top priorities in our American society!" "All parents want their kids to learn!" Those statements sound very good and very believable coming off the lips of a public official who is trying to ingratiate himself with the public. In an ideal world they would be true, but those of us in education don't work in an ideal world; we work in real schools.

I can understand why so many people believe those wonderful words because there is one mistake that I make every year that, no matter how long I teach, I am unable to correct. I do much of my curriculum planning in the summer, and when I do this, I always have too wonderful a world in mind. As the summer progresses, and I get further from the previous year's classroom, the more nearly perfect I picture next year's classrooms. The students I see in my midsummer mind are those who come to class every day and make their education a reasonably high priority. They deal honestly with me, and they all come from homes with concerned, reasonable, and honest parents. The kids who do insanely self-destructive things become only a vague memory. If my summer break lasted any longer, slogans like "No Child Left Behind" might actually begin to sound reasonable. But then September comes, and real students come back to real classrooms, and reality hits me like a cold splash of water in the face. I am reminded that not all students are like the ones I have been imagining during those blissful three months. It doesn't take long before I'm rummaging through my desk, trying to remember where I put the aspirin bottle I used last spring to deal with the headache situations I had so effortlessly put out of my mind.

"Was I Absent Last Week?"

I'm sure parents expect that, when their children come back to school after having been absent, the teachers will welcome them with smiles and open arms. To be perfectly honest, I frequently find it difficult to smile and open my arms! Do I sound like an unfeeling jerk? If so, you probably assume that absent students are absent for good reasons. Let me assure you that, in a depressingly high percentage of cases, you would be wrong.

When I was in school, being sick was just about the only reason I ever missed school. And being sick meant running a fever, or breaking out with measles or chicken pox, or vomiting, or having diarrhea or some combination of those things. A case of the sniffles definitely did not qualify. And from the time I was in kindergarten until the time I graduated from high school I can count on one hand my absences for other things. The reason I remember my absences is because there weren't very many of them.

There are students I've had in class who have actually asked me, "Was I absent last week?" They have to ask because they don't remember, and they don't remember because being absent is no big deal to them. The excuses we see today obviously include illness and, of course, some of those are legitimate. People get viruses, and in the winter the flu is always a problem. I find a student who comes back in January after a three day absence, with "illness" written on the excuse, completely credible, and that student might actually get some sympathy from me. I might wonder when a student misses only one day, but if it's a rare absence for that student, once again, I'll probably be understanding. But when a student misses one day one week for "illness," and then one day the next week, and then one day the week after that, and so on, or if the student's absences regularly fall on test days or on days when important assignments are due, my understanding turns into annoyance. I also have trouble being sympathetic if a boy misses school the morning of a test day for "illness," but then shows up in the afternoon. Whenever one of these guys comes in with the old "morning sickness" excuse, I'm tempted to ask him if he's pregnant.

Illness certainly isn't the only excuse I see. My three favorites are "out of town," "needed at home," and "parent request." Each of these excuses may truly be legitimate, and, in fact, one of my greatest fears is that I will someday make a nasty remark to some student who has such an excuse only to find out that his mother just had major surgery. The reason I find those generic excuses so frustrating is that I see them from the same kids over and over, and I know from experience that they are rarely for something like their mom's surgery.

All of these excuses are considered excused absences because parents wrote them. Some of these parents are trying to be their sons' or daughters' buddies, and they will write excuses for them whenever the child wants one. Parents will also lie for their children if they forgot to study for a test or complete a project that is due. Very often, this results from something I refer to as "good kids' disease." These parents view their own sons and daughters as "good kids," and "good kids" shouldn't have to fail a test for which they forgot to study, and they certainly shouldn't serve detention for an illegitimate absence. Only "bad kids" should have to do that. Apparently these parents don't think that being a "good kid" has much to do with integrity.

There are some other parents who don't see education as being very important, so they just don't think it's a big deal if their children miss school now and then, even twice a week. Warroad is a factory town, and most of the people working in the plant aren't there because they had great academic careers. I worked in the plant during my first summer in Warroad, and many of the workers will tell you that they regret not having tried harder in school, and they truly want their children to do better. Some, however, don't look at it that way. They did not have good experiences in school, so now they have no use for schools in general. These people, when parents of students in our school, are not exactly what you'd call "supportive."

Our school secretaries are usually the ones who have the thankless task of reading notes from parents, and then deciding whether the absences should be excused. Sometimes the excuses are so ridiculous, or the lies so transparent that they mark "unexcused" on the absence slips regardless of the notes. Here's an example: "Please excuse Billy. He wanted to sleep in yesterday."

Refusing to accept notes is no fun, however, because some parents believe *they* have the right to excuse their children for anything, or they should be believed even if they are lying. In fact, they are very offended when the school says, "No!" We are far from perfect, and we make our share of mistakes of commission and especially of omission, but we are honestly trying to do what we can to teach responsible behavior to students. Fighting parents to do it, however, is very difficult.

Every so often, I'll ask a student for her absence slip and see after she hands it to me that it just says "skipped." I don't want students to skip, but at least I can feel a little respect for a student in this situation, because she's either admitted what she's done, or she has a parent who refuses to lie for her. It's the lying and the game playing that are really hard to take.

Adding to the frustration of this is the extra work that is created at the worst possible time. The most important time of any class hour is the very beginning. Getting a class moving in a constructive direction right off the bat sets the tone for the whole hour, but sometimes it's impossible because I'm so busy signing absence slips and digging out assignments for kids who were "out of town," "needed at home," or whatever. I'm also very annoyed by having to spend a portion of my preparation hour correcting make-up assignments that students should have completed a couple of days before. Granted, this isn't a lot of work, and once again, doing these things for students who miss three or four days a year because they were honestly sick is something any teacher willingly accepts. But when I end up doing it over and over for kids who are gone almost weekly, or for kids who are gone only on test days, my tolerance tends to run pretty low.

"Not Me! Honest!"

There is nothing that takes the fun out of teaching like being unable to trust students. Having a disruptive kid on whom I have to keep my eye every second is the worst, but fortunately, there aren't too many of those in our school. There are, however, a lot of students who will cheat whenever it's convenient.

I hate everything about cheating. I hate suspecting that some students might be cheating, I hate thinking students have gotten away with it, and I even hate catching them. Confronting someone I've caught cheating is the most miserable thing I have to do in my role as a teacher. It amounts to saying, "You are a liar," and more often than not, the student to whom I'm saying this is someone with whom I've had a pretty good relationship up to that time. I know that in many cases, as soon as I tell students that I've determined that they've been cheating, it's time to let the lying begin. Some kids will lie regardless of how incontrovertible the evidence, and then I have to go into my ace detective role, which is not a role I enjoy. Students who cheat, however, are not hardened criminals, so their stories usually fall apart rapidly. Here is an example from an interview conducted by our principal, Bill Kirkeby, and me with a student who, after being accused of exchanging answers with another student on a number of quizzes, protested his innocence.

> *Kirkeby: If you weren't cheating, how did you end up with the same answers on all the questions, and the exact same mistake on this question?*
>
> *Student: I don't know.*
>
> *Kirkeby: Did he (the student's friend) give you a little help on this question?*
>
> *Student: Well, actually on that one, I think I helped him.*
>
> *Kirkeby: So, in other words, you do communicate with him during quizzes.*
>
> *Student: Well, he gives me hints once in a while.*
>
> *Fermoyle: How did he know what questions you needed "hints" for?*
>
> *Student: Well, I have a tendency to read the questions out loud.*

In most cases, it's possible to get the student to own up to the cheating or simply drop the claim of innocence without too much trouble, but sometimes it isn't that easy. The worst situations occur when the student goes home and lies to the parent about the incident. When this happens, it becomes much more difficult to get an admission because the student doesn't want to admit to his parent that he lied. This can get very ugly when the parent is one of those who believes her role in dealing with the school is to be an advocate for her child. In this case, once again, it doesn't matter how incontrovertible the evidence is because, as so many parents claim, "My son wouldn't lie to me!"

Every time I confront a student with cheating, I am scared to death that I'm making a mistake. Even when the evidence seems crystal clear, I'm afraid I'm missing something. Maybe I'm ignorant of some set of circumstances or I'm misinterpreting what happened. Maybe I'm accusing someone who hasn't done anything wrong! This fear causes me to avoid making an accusation unless I'm dead sure about it, but even then, I still worry, and this just adds to the misery of dealing with cheating.

Although there is nothing funny about cheating, there often is about the way kids manage to get caught. On numerous occasions, I've caught students cheating on things like essay tests because they wrote notes on their desks, but then forgot to erase the evidence. Dumb! It's always interesting to see the looks on their faces when they're confronted with that evidence. Even when confronted with this smoking gun, kids sometimes deny it and try to explain their way out of it, but they only to manage to sound idiotic. Usually they simply assume a look of shock on their faces; then you can literally see the wheels start to turn in their minds as they try in vain to come-up with a viable explanation. Finally a look of resignation appears. They might not actually admit that they cheated, but they don't argue when told that their grade will be a zero.

The funniest instances of cheaters hanging themselves often take place on my short-answer reading quizzes. I have three or four different sections of the same class, so I make two or three different versions of the same quiz. For example, for a reading assignment about the ratification of the Constitution, the last question on one of the quizzes reads, "Which two states had not yet ratified the Constitution when the new government went into effect?" Answer: North Carolina and Rhode Island. In the next class, the last question will read, "What three men wrote the Federalist papers?" When a student answers that question by writing,

"North Carolina and Rhode Island," as one hapless young man did, I've got a clue.

The most common form of cheating is probably the same one that it's always been—good old fashioned eyeballing. I remember a gruff old English teacher I had in junior high school telling us before a test that if he saw any eyeballs slithering across the halls, he would step on them. The image of that has always stuck with me, so I've plagiarized it and used it at some time in every one of my classes. This threat doesn't stop many of the students who want to cheat, however.

The easiest things to eyeball are answers on multiple choice and matching tests, where it's simply a matter of copying A, B, C or D. A number of years ago, I had one class in which two students, who never seemed to know very much, did amazingly well on a couple of these tests in a row. At that time, I decided to make second versions of my multiple choice tests. The questions would all be the same, but the letters designating the answers would be changed. In other words, on one test the correct answer would be C, but on the other version of the test, it would be B. Ah, the magic of the word processor!

The first time I tried this, the students I was suspicious of had answers that were nearly identical to friends who were sitting next to them, even though they had different tests. There were something like sixty questions on the test, and the students being copied had about two and three wrong, while the guys with the roving eyeballs missed between fifty and fifty-five. When they received back their graded tests, both of them seemed a little confused, but neither of them said anything. Rather than confronting them, I decided to keep it to myself and see what happened on the next test. One of the students did his own work, and ended up with a mediocre score, but the other gave a repeat performance. And he did again on the next one after that. He eventually figured out that eyeballing on those tests wasn't working, but it took him a while and, needless to say, he didn't end up doing very well in the class. Years later, I ran into him after he had graduated from college. (Yes, he actually graduated from college!) He approached me with a shrewd look on his face, and said, "You know, I used to cheat in your class!" What could I say? Some cheaters are clever, but some cheaters are not nearly as clever as they think.

I said earlier that many of the students I accuse of cheating are students with whom I've had good relationships, and that is because cheating is definitely an equal opportunity character flaw. Males are just as likely to cheat as females, whites just as likely as minorities, athletes just as likely as non-athletes, and A and B students every bit as likely as C, D and F students.

As much as I hate cheating, I know that many of those who do it are not really bad people. Not every student cheats, but a lot of them do, and it is definitely part of student culture. Since I began teaching sociology a few years ago as an elective course offered to juniors and seniors, I've had open discussions in the class about cheating.

Students, in general, do not think cheating is terribly wrong. Let's face it, there's a lot going on in our society to lead kids to believe that dishonesty of any kind is not a big deal. Anyone watching TV for any amount of time is besieged by commercials that, though not out and out lies, certainly twist the truth. Truth-twisting has been turned into an art form by politicians and their handlers in political campaigns and advertising. It's not unusual to see someone who is running for or holding public office doing his best to explain why a lie he told is really not a lie at all. Democrats and Republicans are equally shameless when it comes to this, but the ultimate example has to be President Clinton's handling of his Monica Lewinsky mess, and just about all of the students that I've had in class the last few years remember that fiasco.

One of the most talked about events that has taken place on TV in the last ten years was the 2004 Super Bowl half-time show, during which pop star Janet Jackson bared her breast, revealing an interesting piece of artwork on her nipple. The first explanation we heard for that display was that it was a "wardrobe malfunction." Explanations of that explanation followed. Another hot topic has been a steroid investigation in baseball. Some of the athletes who are subjects of this looked like normal baseball players early in their careers, but suddenly became Arnold Schwarzenegger look-alikes. Their typical reaction to any accusations could best be summed up with, "What, me? Steroids? How could you think that?" But a better question might be, "How could a rational person not think that?"

So students see ample evidence that cheating and lying are simply ways to get ahead in life, and if caught, the way to handle the situation is to lie some more. And while many students don't think cheating is a terrible thing to do, they do think that turning in a cheater is. They justify this by saying, "everybody cheats," or "it's none of their business," or that all-time popular favorite, "they're only hurting themselves when they cheat."

I know that this last line is one that young people hear frequently from adults, but I also know it's not true. Students who cheat do hurt others. Most obviously, it may allow the cheater to move ahead of other students in class rank, which is viewed as a crucial factor by most colleges in the admissions process. On a more basic level, if one student has worked hard studying for a test or writing a long paper, and another student who hasn't done the work cheats and gets a better grade, that's going to hurt the morale of the one who put in the effort.

Cheating also hurts everyone because it breaks down trust. I don't know how many times a student or students have done well on a test or some other assignment in my class, and instead of just feeling good about it, I've had lingering doubts in my mind. Why did they do so well? Did they study harder than usual? Did I do a good job teaching it? Or did they cheat? I hate having to think that, but I know from experience that I'm a fool if I don't. More than once I've found out that students for whom I had the utmost respect—students who I thought were completely honest and would never cheat—had, in fact, cheated on a test or an important assignment. This would have shocked me early in my career, but now that I am older I am only mildly surprised.

There are times when a student cannot cheat by himself; he needs help, someone to feed him the answers on a quiz or a test, or to give him a completed assignment to copy. There are students with enough character to tell the cheater to "buzz off" and do his own work, but a determined cheater can always find a willing helper. When this happens, I'm not sure who makes me angrier. I've always thought of cheating as parasitic, but I view helping cheaters as being somewhat like prostitution. The person who helps others cheat has something that no one else has a right to, and it shouldn't be given away, namely, the work that has been done, or the knowledge gained from studying. A prostitute sells her or his body for money, and the student who helps cheaters sells what he has for friendship.

This sounds harsh because I really care about the learning that takes place in my classroom and, whether they know it or not, students who cheat, along with their helpers, take a wrecking ball to what I am trying to build when I teach. The foundation of all of my classes is student effort. There will be some students who are interested in the subject matter from the first day they walk into my class, but I don't want them to be the only ones who do well and enjoy it. I try to hook the average students by making it clear that, if they make a good effort, they can also earn good grades. In trying to earn those good grades, students will learn something. My hope is that, as they learn and gain success, they'll become interested in the subject and they'll be motivated to learn even more. Students who cheat and get away with it destroy that foundation. They may get the good grade, but they haven't done the work for it, and they haven't learned a thing—at least nothing that I wanted them to learn. Their interest in the subject doesn't improve one bit, and they have no incentive to work harder. And when someone gets away with cheating, a lot of other students are going to be tempted to go the same route, especially if the cheater gets a better grade than the kids who were honest.

I know that I shouldn't, but I can't help taking cheating personally. I value my relationship with students, and there is nothing worse for any relationship than dishonesty. When students cheat, they are lying to me. They are telling me they did work that they never did, that they learned something they never learned, that they deserve a grade that they have no business getting. They are trying to pull the wool over my eyes and, in effect, I feel they are trying to make a fool out of me.

I think it's obvious from the amount of cheating that goes on in schools that the consequences of getting caught often aren't harsh enough. A zero on one quiz or one assignment or one test isn't that big a deal to a student if she has gotten away with cheating on enough other things. An obvious solution is for the penalty to be an F for the entire marking period or semester. I had that as a policy when I first came to Warroad, but the reaction from parents was so hostile that I was forced to back off. We had an excellent young teacher come to Warroad a couple years ago who followed that policy as well, and he was praised for his courage, at least as long as the kids who were getting caught were those C or D students who didn't seem to have the greatest attitudes anyway. When a couple of nice A and B students with concerned parents got nailed, however, a lot of the solid support he had enjoyed suddenly turned to Jell-O. Cheating is one of the biggest problems in our high schools today, and until teachers, administrators, honest students, and parents get serious about it, it will continue to be.

"I Had To Work!"

"I couldn't do my homework because I had to work." Every teacher in northern Minnesota has heard this excuse, and I don't think we're alone. I always have to shake my head when I go to my local supermarket and see kids, who never seem to be able to get an assignment done on time, working. I know there are many people who believe that schools should give more homework and be more demanding, but I can assure you that my students who work and their parents are not among them.

Every person is different, but as a parent I wanted my kids to go to school and participate in any extracurricular activities that interested them. I am convinced that's the best route for most students. There are a myriad of different activities offered in our high schools, and I believe that most of the young people who choose not to take advantage of any of them are missing the boat. Taking advantage of those activities doesn't just mean "showing up" for them, either; it means dedicating themselves to be the best they can possibly be at them. High school kids should all try to be good students, and if they are in athletics, they should try to be the best athletes they can be. If they are in choir, they should try to be the best singers. If they are in the school play, then they should try to be the best actors and actresses. There is no way, however, that we can expect teenagers to be focused enough to do their best at those things while working at a part time job during the school year.

I used to think that students should not work during the school year, period! I guess I've mellowed with age. I've come to recognize that there are some young people who have no interest in extracurricular activities, and really no interest in school either. They just want to get out into the working world, and the only reason they are still in school is so they can show their future employers a high school degree. I really believe many of these kids are selling themselves short, but they have to live their lives.

I have also seen a number of students who seem to be able to handle going to school, holding down a part-time job, and perhaps even participating in a less demanding extracurricular activity, and doing all these things well. Frankly, I don't know how they do it. I know how I feel at the end of a school day, and going to another job immediately afterward would be unthinkable. There is no way that I could work as hard at my teaching as I do if I were moonlighting, and I don't think there's a huge difference between trying to be a conscientious teacher and trying to be a conscientious student. Yet, some of my students are able to walk through the school doors in the afternoon and head directly to their part-time jobs with smiles on their faces, yet still consistently manage to have their homework done and get good grades. If a kid can do this, how can I knock it?

But for every young person who is able to keep up with his or her schoolwork while holding a part-time job during the school year, there are several others whose performances clearly suffer. A lot of these kids come from families where parents don't place much importance on education, and that's sad, because some of their children could do well if they ever decided to apply themselves. Many of the working class parents in Warroad don't make an overwhelming amount of money, so there are a few families with teenagers who are working to help the family make ends meet. But that's not usually the case. In fact, I have had this conversation with working students more than once:

Question: "Why do you work during the school year?"
Answer: "So I can pay for my car."
Question: "Well, why do your need a car?"
Answer: "So I can get to work."

Parents who encourage their teenagers to work often claim that this teaches them responsibility. For those students who manage to keep their grades up, this may well be the case. But for the many who are unable to do so, it's hard to see how having them come to school unprepared day after day, with assignments undone and tests not studied for, teaches them to be responsible.

There is one group of students who are definitely hurt by working during the school year, and those are the ones involved in demanding extracurricular activities. As a hockey coach, I know how much commitment playing in our sport requires, and I know how intense our practices and our games are. It takes every ounce of energy and responsibility that a student-athlete can muster to play hockey and perform well in school, and there is almost never a way that someone can also work a part-time job without having something suffer. The physical, mental, and time demands are simply too much, yet we have had some kids try to do it. I can only understand parents condoning this if their child's working is an absolute economic necessity. But don't try arguing that having someone take a part-time job while going to school and participating in something like hockey, football, basketball or volleyball is teaching that person responsibility. Exercising responsibility means doing things well, not cutting every possible corner in order to get by, and this is what these young people have to do.

"She's Not Lazy! She's Got a Disability."

Special education is a wonderful concept. I said earlier that my wife, Susan, had a severe hearing problem when she was a child. If you ever had a short meeting with this very pretty and personable fifty-two-year-old woman, the only sign you'll ever see that she had a problem would be the small hearing aids that she wears. If you spent a little more time with her, however, you might find her mispronouncing simple words, like "symbol" or "success." Susan also never really got some basic English and math concepts because she couldn't hear, but she is bright enough to be able to hide it from almost anyone. As a result, you would have no idea how much this gap in her knowledge bothers her to this day. She could have benefited greatly from extra help for the things she was missing because of her impaired hearing.

We should help children with learning problems, and we should also be aware that some children have legitimate problems, like ADHD and emotional and behavior disorders (EBD). These kids deserve our help, too, and we may have to make some allowances for their behavior. Special education programs have been set up to do this. That's good, and there have been many deserving young people who have been helped by them. However, special education has also become a program for some kids who are more than happy to use their disabilities as excuses for misbehaving and not performing as well as they could.

A meeting we had in our school with parents of an ADHD student a couple of years ago serves as a prime example of how this can happen. I had their daughter in class, and she didn't do one reading assignment during an entire marking period. That's about twenty-five reading assignments and, to top it off, the parents insisted that this girl was a speed-reader. Every teacher at this meeting was convinced that a big part of this girl's problem was that she was very lazy, but her parents insisted she was not. They were adamant on this point because, they told us, the doctor who had diagnosed the girl had emphasized to them that she wasn't lazy. Now, I have never practiced medicine, but I fail to understand how a doctor could see anyone for fifteen minutes or a half hour and make the diagnosis that she's not lazy. I didn't know that laziness was a medical condition!

The parents of the student in this case were responsible people, and I don't doubt that this girl was legitimately diagnosed with ADHD. But I also have no doubt that she was lazy. The doctor may have seen her for an appointment or two, but I saw her in action—excuse me, I should say inaction—for nearly a year. I'm willing to concede that her medical condition could have caused her to miss some of those reading assignments. But all twenty-five? She also never took notes. Did her condition make it impossible for her to do that? Every day? I don't think so. I believe this fairly bright girl used her disability—and her parents concern about it—as an excuse to do nothing. Once she had the authoritative word of a doctor that she wasn't lazy, she had it made in the shade.

It is not unusual for teachers to see this type of situation when dealing with special education. While it is supposed to be a program to help students overcome disabilities, being in a special ed program too often serves as an excuse for students not doing things that teachers believe very strongly they are capable of doing. In fact, some very good parents of children with legitimate learning disabilities don't want their children in special education programs because they're afraid other kids who are in the program will be a bad influence on their children. These parents know that the work habits and behavior of some of those students are horrible. This results in a situation where we have some of the students who could most benefit from special education programs—students for whom they are supposed to exist—not being in them. Instead, we end up spending an unbelievable amount of money, time, manpower, and resources on some kids who make almost no effort to learn.

The key word in dealing with special education students for classroom teachers is "modifications." There are modifications that are perfectly reasonable, like having handouts in larger fonts for students with vision problems. With enough pressure from the parents, however, modifications might be designed to make sure that a special education student will not suffer normal consequences for his lack of effort.

In our high school, teachers turn in weekly lists of failing students. If a student is failing in a class two weeks in a row, that student becomes ineligible for participating in extracurricular activities until he improves his grade. Our ineligibility system has literally saved many students who didn't care very much about academics, but who did the work necessary to pass their classes and graduate because they cared about playing on the football team, the basketball team, or the hockey team.

A few years ago, we had a relatively capable special education student whose modifications included an exclusion from scholastic ineligibility. This attempt to "help a student with a disability" ended up dooming her. In this case, the student was an outstanding singer in the choir, and that was what she really cared about. Her exclusion from scholastic ineligibility was the result of pressure from the parents who were afraid she would miss a couple of concerts if she were restricted from singing because of bad grades. The girl did end up being able to sing in all the choir concerts during her junior year, but the next year she dropped out of school because she was failing several of her classes. In other words, her second year as a junior wasn't going any better than her first. The people in our school should never have agreed to exempt this girl from being scholastically ineligible, but her parents were insistent. Battling them didn't seem worth it, so our school caved in, and in the end the girl was the big loser.

Dealing with students with disabilities has become an increasingly important issue in public education. There has been an amazing proliferation of kids who have one label or another since I began teaching. At the start of my career, there were a few kids who were in special education, but now there are many more. There are also a number of kids who do not qualify for special education, but are given a learning disability label that qualifies them for something called 504 plans. The number of kids who are labeled ADHD and EBD has increased, and recently there have been more and more students diagnosed with other mental or emotional problems like depression and bipolar disorder. If there were as many kids with these problems when I went to school as there seem to be now, and they all went unmedicated and untreated, I have to wonder why most of my classes didn't resemble scenes from *One Flew Over the Cuckoo's Nest*. In other words, there are so many kids who are labeled today that it's hard to believe that all of them really should be.

Whether or not the label is legitimate, the important thing is how the student who is said to have a disability approaches his education. Once again, the key is usually the attitude of the parents. If the parents view the disability as an obstacle to be overcome rather than as an excuse to be used when convenient, and if they assume the school has the best interest of the student at heart, the chances that the student will make a good effort and be successful are high. Over the years I have met with hundreds of parents who understood that, and we've been able to work together for the good of their children. Two of my most rewarding experiences in teaching were seeing an educable mentally handicapped student earn a straight A in one of my basic classes by recording a score of ninety-eight percent on a two-day final test of over 150 questions, and seeing a legitimately labeled EBD student become a positive leader in one of my other basic classes.

There is a lot today that discourages parents from taking that positive approach, however. Whenever I have searched the Internet for items dealing with special education, I have inevitably run into websites sponsored by advocates for students with disabilities that seemingly screamed to parents, "KNOW YOUR RIGHTS!" These websites imply to parents that public schools are very anxious to leave their children behind. When I attend an individual education plan (IEP) or 504 meeting with parents who have been influenced by this kind of thinking, I know that when it comes to their child, it's going to be a long year.

Contrary to what some "advocates" would have parents believe, teachers and schools are willing to make reasonable modifications to help students with disabilities as long as the students are willing to make an honest effort. When parents view themselves as advocates and teachers as the enemy, however, the chances increase that the child will view his disability as an excuse, and his effort will be a lot less than it could be.

"The American People Blah, Blah, Blah..."

If you haven't already noticed, the common thread that connects all of my complaints is the complicity of adults, usually parents. The public pronouncements of politicians and others about public education paint a scenario in which all people outside of the education system seem flawless. We hear things like, "The American people demand that our schools have high standards," or, "All parents want a first rate education for their children." Whether the speaker is a Republican like George W. Bush or a Democrat like Hillary Clinton, he or she makes it sound as if the public in general, and parents in particular, are willing to bear any burden, support any friend, and oppose any foe in order to bring about a better education for our nation's children. The implication is that any educational problems we have are the fault of teachers and administrators who aren't working hard enough. They aren't doing what "the American people" want. To that I say, "Balderdash!"

It is understandable that politicians trying to win votes would speak in glowing generalities, but it's frustrating for those of us who have to deal with reality. When it comes to supporting education, my community is definitely better than average, but it is a long way from fitting into the scenario painted by those politicians. It is a fact that a lot of adults don't place a very high priority on education, and there are others who support strict behavioral and academic standards most of the time, but not in situations when they might inconvenience their own children.

Public schools are dependent upon the people in their communities for support, so they try very hard to keep as many of them as possible happy. This is especially true when school districts need to pass referendums in order to avoid having to make massive cuts. Parents who allow their children to miss school with alarming frequency and parents who take their kids on weeklong vacations to Florida in the middle of the school year don't support high attendance standards. Neither does the employer in one of our neighboring communities who encouraged his teenaged workers to skip their afternoon classes so they could work more. I think it's safe to assume that parents, who allow their teenagers to take part-time jobs during the school year when their grades are mediocre or failing, aren't particularly interested in having higher academic standards. Some of those "advocates" for special education students and some of those students' parents seem to want academic and behavioral standards to be as low as possible. Finally, those parents who don't want their children to face any meaningful consequences after they've been caught cheating may want their kids to get good grades, but they certainly don't want high integrity standards. Most of these people vote, and many of them are willing to call principals and buttonhole school board members to complain when they feel that schools have been too demanding. These people have a very real effect on public schools. The politicians' platitudes make it seem as if these people don't exist, but public schools can't afford to pretend that that is the case.

There are adults who really are like the ones portrayed by our politicians, but not all of them are. If they were, we wouldn't be hearing about such low test scores, and we wouldn't be hearing about such high dropout rates, and we probably wouldn't have "experts" on TV calling our public education system a national disgrace. Yes, there are problems in public education, but it's important to realize that sometimes those problems are the result of public schools giving in to "the American people" and allowing them to get exactly what they want.

Reform to the Left

There are many "experts" out there who have plans to improve our public school system, and there is nothing new in that. The attempts to reform public education have been going on for more than a century. Today reformers have all sorts of different ideas. On one end of the spectrum are the "progressives," who seem to think that too many teachers are old-fashioned in their teaching methods. They believe that the way to improve education lies in changing teaching techniques in order to reach the kids who are performing poorly. On the other side of the spectrum are conservatives who believe that teachers and teachers' unions are the biggest problem, and that our educational system as it is now is hopelessly under their control. They see incompetent or disgustingly lazy teachers who are protected by their unions everywhere, and they think the only way to fix education is to force public schools to compete with private schools by using something like a voucher system.

There aren't very many teachers who agree with conservatives, but there are some teachers who are willing to become true believers in the latest progressive reforms. Many others, however, have turned into lifetime reform-cynics. No field seems to breed as many acronyms as education, and our reform-cynics have their own batch. TYNT stands for "This Year's New Thing," while LYNT stands for "Last Year's New Thing." President Bush believes that his NCLB stands for "No Child Left Behind," but our reform-cynics, who have seen reform after reform come and go, refer to it as "New Crap Like Before."

It might sound terrible that teachers would be so cynical, but it's hard not to be. In the early 1990's, we were told that all schools in Minnesota would have to convert to outcome-based education. The old timers in our school said, "It'll never happen." They were right—it never did. A few years later we were going to convert to something called Minnesota's Profiles of Learning, which was inspired by the latest progressive reforms, and we spent hours and days in workshops listening to presenters expound on the wisdom of this new system. We were all supposed to design complicated project-type activities in which students would demonstrate mastery by "doing" something. We'd then rate those students on a one-to-four scale, rather than on the traditional A, B, C, D, F model. Do you understand that? Neither did we. And neither did the different presenters at those workshops. "Never fear," our old-timers told us, "this too shall pass." Mercifully, it has.

Our state's most recent stroke of educational reform genius is the Minnesota Academic Standards. This is more in the educational traditionalist mode, and it just proves that educational progressives don't have a monopoly on bad ideas. When I learned what the Standards required for American history, it almost made me long for the days of the Profiles of Learning. The state now wants me to overwhelm my students with a massive amount of material—something similar to what I did when I first began teaching American history. I quit teaching that way because it didn't work very well. I figured out that trying to cover too much makes it impossible to go into depth about anything, and most students end up understanding and remembering very little. Nevertheless, the state of Minnesota wants me to go back to that. If I do what they are telling me to do, I'm afraid more than a few of my students won't learn who we fought in the Revolutionary War. Oh, we'll cover it all right, but we'll have to rush through it because of the time I'll have to spend doing things like explaining the differences between Mayan and Aztec architecture.

Many teachers look upon reforms so negatively because some of them are foolish, and also because so many have come and gone. But I really believe another important reason for the resistance is that these ideas, whether they are considered progressive or traditional, are usually promoted by people who argue that public education in America is horrible. "Failing" is the word they love to use. I don't accept that we're failing, and I get angry every time I hear someone say that we are. If someone shows me something and tells me that it might help to make me a more effective teacher, I might be reluctant to change my ways, but I'll listen. If I am told to throw out everything I'm doing, and to start all over because I'm a failure, I find it hard to keep an open mind.

Education's Edsel

I first became aware of progressive educational reform during the last week of my senior year in high school. Our Modern Problems teacher told us about a new program they were going to implement the following year called "modular scheduling." Rather than consisting of the normal fifty-five-minute class periods we had always known, the school day would be divided up into twenty-minute mods. Instruction would be given in classes that would last either one mod (twenty minutes) or two mods (forty minutes). The students wouldn't be taking any more classes than we had been taking, so they would have a great deal of additional time to work on their own.

This was a classic example of an educational reform whose promoters must have been astonishingly naive about high school students. It didn't take the kids in our Modern Problems class long to figure out that, under this system, the students would all have the equivalent of two to three hours of study hall. I think the term the experts used was something like "independent study," but we knew better. And we also knew how we liked to spend our study hall time. Most of us used some of our study hall time to do homework, but we spent much of the time playing games such as Hangman. We all knew that the typical high school student would never use two to three hours of "independent study" time effectively.

Modular scheduling became the rage across the state of Minnesota in the early seventies, and some schools actually combined that idea with an "open campus," in which students could come and go as they pleased. Guess what most of them did with their independent study time then?

When I went to do my student teaching at a Minneapolis suburban high school four years after I'd first heard about modular scheduling, the faculty was voting to euthanize it. It wasn't long before modular scheduling went the way of the Edsel throughout the state of Minnesota. It seems very clear that, although the eighteen-year-olds in my graduating class could all figure out that modular scheduling was doomed to failure, the educational geniuses who guided policy couldn't. I think this says a lot about educational reform. There is nothing wrong with exploring new ideas, but schools should be very careful about overhauling their systems just because "the experts" recommend it.

Panaceas They Aren't

I can't think of anything positive that came out of modular scheduling, but in fairness, many other progressive educational reforms have some good points. From 1999 through 2001, I took classes in order to earn a Masters Degree, and during this time I became familiar with a number of more recent "progressive" reforms. I learned the jargon, and I could write outcomes (instead of objectives), and create performance assessments (instead of tests), and devise a rubric (instead of a grade scale). I knew about brain-based learning (kind of makes you wonder what other learning is based on, doesn't it?), and I could "wow" my principal in a discussion about the Minnesota Profiles of Learning. (Neither of us really understood them, but I was better able to pretend that I did.) Although I could see the value of many of the ideas I learned about, I never became a true believer.

If there is any one idea that has been at the heart of recent progressive reforms, I would say that it is Howard Gardner's multiple intelligences theory. This theory says that people have varying abilities in eight different mental areas. According to Gardner, schools have traditionally aimed instruction at the "verbal-linguistic" and "mathematical-logical" intelligence areas, and a lot of people aren't strong in them. His point is that we should be doing more to reach people who are strong in the other areas: spatial (artistic), musical, interpersonal, intra-personal, bodily kinesthetic, and naturalist.

I do think there is something to the idea of multiple intelligences, partially because I see it so much in my own marriage. If you want someone with whom to discuss theories or who can draw logical conclusions from certain information (i.e., a person who is strongly verbal-linguistic and mathematical-logical), I'm your man. My wife? Forget it! But if you want someone to negotiate for you when you want to buy a new car (i.e., someone who is strongly interpersonal), she can save you hundreds or even thousands of dollars. I don't know how many times I've seen her wrap salesmen around her little finger. I, on the other hand, am a sales-person's dream. If every customer were like me, there would be a lot of salespeople who would be able to retire very early.

Although knowing about multiple intelligences can be helpful, it's not a panacea. True believers in multiple intelligences would tell us that students don't perform because we haven't reached out to their strong area of intelligence. That might sound good, but any teacher knows that there are some students who make a good effort no matter what you do in class, and some who don't. The students who don't read assignments and don't take notes are usually the same students who lay their heads on their desks during a video. They are also the ones who object to learning in any different way if it involves any work at all.

Cooperative learning is another tactic that progressives strongly en-courage, and it can be effective. There are some students who respond better when placed into a small group, and high performers often gain an even greater understanding of material by having to explain it to lower performers. Besides that, I know that my kids enjoy having breaks from the old "assignment-lecture-test" routine.

But cooperative learning is no cure-all for our educational problems either. Most of the lowest performers in my classes have done no better in cooperative learning than they have when working individually. While it's very rewarding to see higher performing students trying to help other kids learn, it is discouraging to see that the lowest performing kids are often so lazy that learning is impossible, and they turn out to be giant albatrosses around the necks of the students who are stuck with them in their groups.

One year I had one of these low performing students whom we will call Charles. Charles dropped out to go to our alternative learning center halfway through the year, and about two weeks later, the groups in my class were discussing conservative philosophies of the late nineteenth century. (I know how boring that sounds, but we've actually had some great debates in my classes on that topic over the years.) One of those philosophies was Social Darwinism, which said, among other things, that government should not help the poor because society will become better as the weakest members are eliminated. As the students were working out their positions, the members of Charles' old group suddenly burst out laughing. When I asked them what was so funny, one of the members told me, "We believe in Social Darwinism. We've been doing great ever since Charles left!"

Along with multiple intelligences and cooperative learning, educational progressives also promote the use of research projects. James Loewen epitomizes "the expert" who tells teachers—in this case, history teachers—that we are doing almost everything wrong. In his book, *Lies My Teacher Told Me*, he argues that the misguided way we've been teaching American history to generations should be corrected by using what progressives refer to as "the inquiry method." That basically means that we should have our students engage in a series of projects; they would do research and learn history and draw conclusions on their own.[12] This sounds great, especially to someone who is used to working with college students rather than high school kids. Loewen says that he has observed high school classes, but this is not the same as teaching those classes day after day after day.

My own experience with research projects as a student makes me very skeptical about the inquiry method. When I have approached research projects with a high degree of background knowledge and motivation, I've found doing them valuable. This was the case when I was working for my Masters Degree, and even when I was working on something in my major field in college. On the other hand, when I did research projects involving things about which I initially knew or cared little—like ones I did when I was in high school—the results were unimpressive. And believe me, when it comes to background knowledge and motivation, the great majority of the high school kids I teach are a lot more like I was in high school than the way I was when I was working for my Masters.

12. Loewen, *Lies my teacher told me*, 309-310

My son tells a story about an incident when he was a student in my class that illustrates the background knowledge of some kids. It was February, and we had covered the period from 1492-1914 in American history, so we had studied the Revolutionary and Civil Wars, among others, and were now talking about World War I. A frustrated young man sitting in front of my son turned to him and asked, "When are we finally going to get to those wars that Conan fought in?" If I'd have taught the First World War by having my class choose topics and conduct "research" on them, this young man would have had no idea where to begin, and he'd probably have no idea where he was when he finished.

I do make some use of projects and research in my social studies classes, but I cannot buy into the idea of basing an entire class on them. In one of my graduate school classes, an American history teacher who did just that was held up as a model for the rest of us to follow. He based his class on student reports and rarely lectured. His students would learn about a unit by researching a topic from it, giving a report to the class on it, and then listening to other students give reports on other topics from the unit.

After hearing about him I had to wonder: was my experience as a student that much different from everybody else's? I asked that because I remember being bored stiff listening to other students give reports. Listening to some kid read from a paper in a monotone, mispronouncing every other word, just didn't turn me on. Some students might learn something from their own research, but I can't believe they enjoy listening to the other kids give their reports, unless this teacher has students who are unusually good at this exercise. If that's the case, and this teacher believes his kids are learning, I'd never tell him to change. But please, don't try to force me to adopt his methods.

Multiculturalism: Changing What We Teach

While multiple intelligences, cooperative learning, and the inquiry method all have to do with instructional methods, multiculturalism is a progressive educational trend that has more to do with content. Multiculturalists believe traditional American history curriculum has placed far too much emphasis on the contributions of white males, and not nearly enough on the contributions of women and minorities.

There is no question that women and minorities have made significant but unacknowledged contributions to our history that deserve our attention. Just as students should know about people such as George Washington, Alexander Hamilton, and Abraham Lincoln, they should also know about people like Tecumseh, Harriet Tubman, and Frederick Douglass. Just as they should know about Franklin Roosevelt, Dwight D. Eisenhower, and Ronald Reagan, they should also know about Booker T. Washington, Martin Luther King, Jr., and Sandra Day O'Connor. Multiculturalists also legitimately draw attention to the way history classes in the past have glorified Columbus and many of the early explorers while at the same time overlooking their despicable treatment of anyone who wasn't white and Christian. American Indians have a point when they say that asking them to celebrate Columbus Day is like asking Jews to celebrate the Holocaust.

I agree with multiculturalists who say that we shouldn't whitewash American history, but I can't go along with the extremists in that movement who seem to want me to present our history solely as a story of oppression by white males. Multicultural extremists believe teachers should emphasize to minority groups and girls not only that they have been oppressed, but also that they are still being oppressed. In fact, one author even argues that anorexia is the result of a plot by white males to hold back the gains that women have made.[13] Such an approach completely ignores the progress that has been made in race and gender relations. It also seems to me that one of the least healthy ways to deal with being a member of a minority group is to blame all one's problems on one's minority status. It is a fact of human nature that if you give someone an excuse for failing before he or she has even tried, the chances of their actually failing goes up greatly. Failure becomes a self-fulfilling prophecy. I don't see how this will contribute to anyone's educational success.

Going Off the Deep End

The problem with progressive reforms is that the true believers end up taking them way too far. Some of their ideas seem downright loony. As I said earlier, I think the multiple intelligences theory has something to it,

---

13. Grant, C.A. & Sleeter, C.E. (1999). *Making choices for multicultural education.* Columbus, Ohio: Prentice Hall, 193

but when someone tells me that the way to make a chemistry class come alive is by having one student dress up like a potato and worship another student who's dressed up like an Aztec sun god, they lose me.[14]

"We must have all our children become self-directed, lifelong learners," the progressives say, so grades and honor rolls shouldn't matter. Those are wonderful goals, but grades and honor rolls can be used to help students get there. A few years ago, I had a girl who was very capable, but she would do only enough to keep her head above water. She earned a C- the first marking period, and a D the second. Her mother then came for a conference, and it was clear after we talked about the class and her daughter's performance that she was disgusted. After that conference, the daughter began to do the class assignments in order to get her mother off her back. I remember her coming into the class one day and looking at the wall where the grades were posted. She sat down with a shocked look on her face, and said, "I'm really doing well!" She became a consistently good student in the class after that, earning a B+ the third marking period and an A- the fourth. In the process, she actually began to enjoy the class and become interested in the subject. She contributed to class discussions, and actually seemed to care about the things we argued about. All this began when she realized she could earn a good grade instead of her usual mediocre or poor grade. In other words, the grade was the hook. If I had waited for her to "learn to love learning for its own sake," I'd still be waiting.

When the disciples of progressive reforms go off the deep end, they give all of us in education the reputation of being a bunch of crackpots. They say things like, "let's eliminate all the disciplines (English, social studies, math, science, etc.)," "we must eliminate all competition from our classrooms," "we must do away with all pencil and paper tests," and "classrooms must never be set up so that the desks are in straight rows." They dismiss certain teaching methods, such as giving textbook reading assignments and lecturing, as hopelessly out of date and completely ineffective. I use both of those methods when I think it's appropriate, and I'm not about to throw them out of my routine. The progressive true believers who criticize the use of lecturing also fail to distinguish between lecturers. As a student, I have had lecturers who could put me to sleep in

14. Kohl, H. (1969). *The open classroom*. New York: New York Review, 65-66

about five minutes, but I've also had great lecturers who made me sorry to see a class come to an end. Should they quit lecturing?

A Progressive's Idea of a Balanced Approach

It's hard to listen to progressive reformers for very long without coming to the conclusion that they want teachers to promote a liberal political agenda. I am somewhere in the middle of the political spectrum, and I wouldn't dream of pushing my views on my students. Not only do I think it would be unethical, but I am also never certain that my own views are correct.

James Loewen may have a point when he complains that history has too often been slanted to promote patriotism, but that doesn't mean it would be right (no pun intended) to promote the liberal or ultraliberal agenda that he favors. Yes, Loewen does say more than once in *Lies My Teacher Told Me* that he favors a balanced approach to teaching history and that students should be taught to think for themselves. But it's really hard to buy this when he says early in the book that, if history had been taught correctly, the public wouldn't have put up with what he strongly implies were the racist policies of the Reagan-Bush years.[15] It might be all right for a college professor to promote this position in his classroom, because his students are expected to be reasonably well informed, but it would be totally inappropriate for a high school teacher to do the same thing. Loewen doesn't seem to understand this.

Loewen's book is full of criticism of textbook publishers and high school teachers for slanting and simplifying complex historical issues, for making all American presidents heroes, and by always making the United States morally good and right. It would be hard for any teacher to slant and simplify history more than Loewen does in his analysis of what he calls his "Vietnam Exercise."[16] Loewen uses the Vietnam War to try to prove that our education system actually makes people "dumber," as he puts it, when it comes to making foreign policy decisions. He uses a 1971 poll in which sixty percent of college-educated people favored pulling out of Vietnam, while eighty percent of people who had only a grade school education also favored pulling out.

15. Loewen, *Lies my teacher told me,* 19

16. Ibid., 297-304

Because most people now view the Vietnam War as having been a mistake, Loewen jumps to the conclusion that anyone who opposed pulling out of that war in 1971 was "dumb." Nowhere in his argument does he acknowledge the complexity of the issues involved in the Vietnam War, or the possibility that someone who thought we shouldn't pull out in 1971 might have been right. After all, two years later in this twelve-year war, we were able to withdraw under a cease-fire that might have given the South Vietnamese government a chance to survive had it not been for Watergate and the collapse of the Nixon administration. By 1971, we had lost about 50,000 troops in the Vietnam War. Was it unreasonable for people answering that poll to hate the idea of those men dying for nothing? Was it unreasonable to worry about what might happen to the South Vietnamese people, who were on the same side as we were, if we pulled out?

In his "Vietnam Exercise," Loewen asked audiences to predict the results of the poll before showing them the actual results. Most of the people who did this exercise said that they thought that more college educated people than grade school educated would have been in favor of pulling out. So did I! Loewen berates us for that, too. How could we be so stupid? "Non-thinking" is the term he actually uses. He says the answer should have been obvious, if we had only thought a little bit. Our foolishness, he explains, is due to the fact that we wrongly assume education makes us more informed, and that high school textbooks understate "the progressive elements of the working class."[17] He doesn't acknowledge the possibility that we might have thought college-educated people were most against the war because most of the demonstrations against the war took place on college campuses. He doesn't mention anything about the "hard-hat demonstration" that took place in favor of the war during the Nixon years in New York, a demonstration that ended up with construction workers beating up college antiwar protesters. Nope, that's not why I got it wrong. I got it wrong because of those darned high school textbooks!

The problems we have in public education today have little if anything to do with which teaching methods and textbooks we use, and they certainly are not caused by the degree to which kids have been taught to

17. Ibid., 303

be patriotic. Low performing students don't do poorly because they've been given too many reading assignments, or have had to listen to too many lectures. They don't do poorly because they've had their feelings hurt by doing poorly in competition, or because they've been sitting in straight rows, or because they've had to take too many pencil and paper tests. Low-performing students generally do poorly because they don't try very hard. There are a lot of progressive ideas that have some merit, and if we take them with a grain of salt, they can help us. If they are used correctly, they can benefit all students, and there might even be a handful of previously unmotivated kids who will be motivated by them. For the most part, however, those who do well in a traditional classroom are going to be the same ones who do well in a progressive one. And if we ever turn exclusively to the methods the progressives promote, throwing out all traditional methods of teaching, our education will end up being worse instead of better.

Reform to the Right

Educational progressives are sometimes misguided, teachers like me believe, but at least they don't seem to be hostile to public education. Our critics from the right, however, believe our public education system is so bad that drastic actions are called for. Many of us who are involved in public education fear that their proposals will destroy public education or at least leave the system unrecognizable. While these critics might claim that their ideas are meant to improve public education, many of them have no qualms about their hostility toward teachers and especially teachers' unions. It is difficult for someone like me to see them as anything other than the enemy.

Accountability?

Many public school critics complain that schools and teachers have not been held accountable for their work. When those of us in education resist accountability proposals, many people assume that it is because we are doing a poor job, and we don't want anyone to know it. But many of us who work in public schools can prove that we're not afraid of accountability—we are coaches.

When Albert Hasbargen, Tim Oshie, and I send our hockey team out on the ice, we know that we are going to be held accountable. Our success or failure will be measured by such things as wins and losses, goals for and goals against, power play and penalty kill percentages, and championships. We know that knowledgeable people in the stands (and those who think they're knowledgeable) will judge every visible decision that we make. The same is true for anyone who coaches any athletic team, and similar standards apply for those who advise knowledge bowl and speech teams, put on school plays, and conduct choir and band concerts. Believe me, those of us involved in these activities are not afraid of being held accountable for our work.

Nevertheless, my own coaching experiences are instructive as to why so many teachers are nervous about being held accountable according to state and national standards. During the winter of 1979-80, I coached a high school hockey team in Mt. Iron that didn't win a game. Nevertheless, my reputation as a coach was actually enhanced because, despite our poor record, many people in the area thought I did a good job managing the team. They knew that we had very young players and that our practice situation was terrible. There was no arena in Mt. Iron, so we were one of the only high school teams in Minnesota who had to practice outside. When the season was over, no one demanded that I be fired, and an area newspaper even ran an editorial praising me. If I had been held to some kind of state or national standard, however, I undoubtedly would have been labeled a "failing" coach.

During the winter of 2004-05, the Warroad High School hockey team that Hasbargen, Oshie and I coached went undefeated and won a state championship. I think we did a good job coaching, but the major reason for the team's success was that we had incredibly talented and highly motivated players. We also had an ideal practice situation in one of the finest arenas in the state. Our team's going undefeated didn't necessarily mean that Hasbargen, Oshie and I were great coaches, just as going winless for a season in Mt. Iron didn't mean that I was a failure.

The same type of situation is true for teachers and schools. Some of them are working in ideal situations with highly motivated students. Others are working in horrible conditions with large numbers of students who don't care about their education. This can even be the case within a community. If you wanted to evaluate me by measuring the learning of some of those great classes that I described in Chapter 2, I'd tell you to be my guest. But on the other hand, if you told me you were going to judge me according to certain other classes I've taught, I'd run away in terror.

If you want to know what kind of teacher someone is, ask her principal, ask the teachers she works with, and ask her students and their parents. If you want to test her students and include the results in the mix of data, go ahead. But don't base an evaluation of that teacher or her school solely on the results of tests given by some government authority who is totally detached from the situation with which that teacher and school is actually dealing.

The teachers in our school would have no qualms about being held accountable if someone proposed a reasonable way to see if we are doing our jobs effectively. But the accountability that is being proposed by our national educational reform plan, No Child Left Behind, is not reasonable. On close examination, the purpose of accountability in No Child Left Behind looks suspiciously like a justification for the future widespread use of vouchers. It requires schools to make adequate yearly progress on state set academic standards, or face being labeled "failing schools" and having sanctions placed upon them. That, in itself, might sound reasonable, but by 2014, schools are expected to have one hundred percent of their students proficient. One hundred percent; otherwise, they are labeled as failing schools! Schools are expected to get even the most apathetic students to pass those tests. All of them! Once again, those of us in public education are being told that we must make kids learn whether they like it or not. And if they don't, it doesn't matter how hard we've tried, or what we've done—the student isn't responsible, we are. The bottom line is that, unless this policy is changed, nearly every school in the nation will eventually be labeled "failing." And as the number of failing schools increases, so will the volume of the cries from our right wing critics for vouchers. If that's accountability, it's the last thing public education needs.

Taking Away the Cream of Our Crop

One of the favorite solutions for those who think public schools are hopeless and that the teachers and teachers' unions have made them that way is "school choice," usually under the form of vouchers. The idea of vouchers originally came from Milton Friedman in an essay that he wrote in 1955. Friedman is a Nobel Prize-winning economist, and this, of course, makes him an expert on education. For some reason, whenever I hear a conservative say the name, "Milton Friedman," I feel like I'm supposed to genuflect.

Friedman would like to change the way education is funded in a way that would encourage families to send their children to private schools. As it is now, our school district in Warroad receives about $6,000 in state aid for every student who attends our high school. If a family in our district chooses to send their child to a private school, we lose the state aid, and the parents are on their own when it comes to paying tuition. Under Friedman's vision, the state aid would go directly to the student and his family in the form of a voucher. They would then be able to spend it on the school of their choice—public or private. So if a student from Warroad wanted to attend St. Thomas Academy in Mendota Heights, Minnesota, the voucher would cover $6,000 of the tuition.

The voucher system has been used in Milwaukee, Cleveland, and other cities, and, so far, test results have been unclear about whether or not the voucher students have benefitted academically. In *Breaking Free*, however, Sol Stern gives a glowing view of vouchers at work, and he raves about the performance of kids in private schools. He seems to expect that his readers will fall over from shock, because some of those kids who are doing well are lower-class or black.[18] But when a student of any race or social class is motivated, and he is put into classes with other motivated students because they come from homes with parents who are willing to pay for their education, why should we be surprised when he does well?

Sociologists tell us that social class does have an influence on whether or not a particular student is motivated. This begins with parents transmitting their values to their children. Upper-middle-class kids are the most likely to have parents who view education as important, and lower-class kids, because of the sense of hopelessness that often accompanies poverty, are the least likely. But that isn't always the case. There are lower-class parents who, despite the difficulties they face, make their children's

18. Stern, *Breaking free*, 175

education a priority. I assume that those who bother to use vouchers to send their kids to private schools are such parents. As I said earlier, students with parents who put a high priority on education usually do well. One thing that can hold them back is getting stuck in classes with kids who can destroy their education, but that shouldn't happen in a private school. There is every reason to expect these kids to be successful if they are placed in a healthy educational setting. The fact that overall test results haven't matched Stern's glowing reports makes me wonder what kind of private schools some of those voucher kids are attending.

When lower-class and minority kids are successful in private schools, Stern credits that to the teachers in those schools. He considers them to be incredibly dedicated—much more so than public school teachers. Many of them, he tells us, have not gone through the normal certification process that public school teachers have to go through, and he implies that this actually makes them better.[19] First of all, the fact that some of those teachers haven't been certified gives me a clue about why voucher students, as a whole, aren't blowing away their public school counterparts on test scores, but Stern has missed another key point: the teachers he praises are working in an ideal situation. Teaching is fun when you get to work with motivated kids. Teaching is fun when you don't have to put up with disruptive students. I can't imagine how teachers working in a situation like that could have anything but high morale.

The major argument you hear from teachers' unions and the Democratic party against vouchers is that they divert valuable resources (namely, money) away from public schools. I don't like it either when school budgets get cut, because I've seen so many good young teachers lose their jobs because of cuts in the past. Losing money, however, is not my main concern. What I am most afraid of losing are those valuable students who have the capability of making our classes better.

Vouchers are a problem and an overall danger for public education because public schools need those voucher students if they are going to improve. Every time a motivated student from a family with parents who care about education is taken out of a public school, it becomes less likely that that school will be successful. And those are exactly the kids

19. Ibid., 199

who we will be losing: kids who can inspire other students to join class discussions, kids who can make cooperative learning groups work, kids who have an uncanny ability to ask the right questions, and kids whose wonderful work ethic rubs off on others.

Due to the fact that public schools are forced to tolerate kids who can make learning impossible for their classmates, I can't argue against vouchers when a school is very bad, and there is little hope that it can ever improve significantly. I have no desire to see motivated students forced to go to a school where the educational odds are hopelessly stacked against them. Rather than having a positive effect on their classmates, it seems more likely that they would lose their own motivation in a bad school. I believe that because I have had classes—thankfully, very few—in which this has happened. It's entirely possible that in a bad school, the loss of motivated students, which concerns me so much, would turn out to be a non-factor, but this isn't the case with potentially good schools.

People like Sol Stern argue that "school choice" will actually benefit public schools, because competition with private schools is the only thing that will force us to get better. What bothers me most about that argument is that the people who make it want us to compete with the equivalent of one hand tied behind our backs. I recently had a talk with someone who had been teaching in a private school in Minnesota for about ten years. I asked him how that school dealt with disruptive students. He told me that if a kid got into trouble, he might get warned, but he might also get kicked out immediately. There would definitely not be a second warning. I then asked him if kids could get kicked out for not doing their schoolwork. He said, "Oh yeah, if they don't keep their grades up, they're gone!"

Why don't Milton Friedman, Sol Stern, Peter Brimelow, and their merry band of conservatives who are so big on the idea of competition ever propose that public schools be given that kind of power? Is it because courts have ruled that we can't do that? Well, it wasn't so long ago that courts were ruling that vouchers used for religious schools violated the separation of church and state. They sure didn't let court rulings stop them from fighting that battle.

I believe in competition, but in order for it to be a good thing, the "players" must have a reasonable chance of winning. If those of us in public schools are going to have to give due process to every malcontent, and pay for the education of disruptive students no matter what they do wrong, I've got news for you—we can't win! If conservatives really want us to compete with private schools, then they should fight to give us the same powers that private schools have in dealing with students.

Homeschooling: A Blessing and a Curse

In Warroad, we actually haven't had to worry too much about competing with private schools. If parents want to send a child to a private school, they'll have to send her to some place like Minneapolis or St. Paul, which are 370 miles away. We've lost some, and the students we've lost have been good ones, but we haven't lost many. We have been hit hard by another growing anti-public school trend in recent years, however: homeschooling.

Homeschooling has gotten a great amount of favorable press, and more and more people are choosing this option for their children. Reports tell about how well many homeschooled kids do on ACTs and SATs, and when a homeschooler won the national spelling bee a couple of years ago, he received a lot of attention. With public education being portrayed as a disaster in the media, homeschooling must look very attractive to a lot of parents.

We have two kinds of homeschoolers in Warroad, and those students in one of them definitely won't be winning any spelling bees or dazzling us with their college entrance exam scores. A typical example is a boy I had at the beginning of a recent school year. He showed up the first day, missed the next two, then showed up again, then missed, and so on. I can't remember all of his excuses, but I do remember one was the ever-popular, "My grandfather's sick." Who knows? Maybe he was. But why a high school student would have to miss eight days for Grandpa's illness is beyond me. In any case, after about three weeks, our school secretary showed me a note from his mother: "I will be homeschooling my son for his last two cources." Her spelling, not mine. Her son's last two "cources" were the American history class that I teach and—you guessed it—English.

Actually, I am all for homeschooling this type of student. Unless he was suddenly transformed, he wasn't going to contribute anything positive to his classes, and he had the definite potential for dragging another student or two down with him. I think our school actually owes that mother a big thank you.

There are other homeschoolers in our district, though, who will do well on college entrance exams. I have no doubt that, with an intelligent parent, a child can get a great education at home. There are valid questions about what a homeschooler misses socially, but from the point of view of a student's academic development, having an individually tailored curriculum could certainly be an advantage.

My biggest concern with homeschooling, as far as motivated students are concerned, is not what they are missing out on, but what our schools are missing out on by not having them with us. We need those kids! While I wrote this book, I had one such student in my economics and sociology classes. He had been homeschooled for most of his life, but he took some classes at our high school. He was a great kid who was very bright, and there could be no doubt that his parents had done a fantastic job. He was a very mild mannered young man, but he took part in our discussions—almost reluctantly, it seemed—and he always had something intelligent to say. My economics and sociology classes were better because of him. I don't know what he missed by not taking all his classes in our schools, but I know that we missed him. I would have loved to have had him in one of my American history classes two years before, and the other students would have loved having him, too. Had he been in one of those classes, that class would have been better, and the students in that class would have learned more.

It would be hard to criticize parents who homeschool their children in a school district that isn't very good, but ours definitely does not fit into that category. We have a school where students can get a good education, because we still have enough kids from families with parents who care about education and who still trust us enough to send us their kids. But if a school like ours loses enough of those kids—as the media, many experts, and politicians seem to be encouraging—it won't matter how good the teachers are, or how good the principal is, or what new and nifty teaching techniques are being used, or how much high tech equipment is brought in. It's simply not going to be a very good place to learn.

Any appeal I make in this respect may well fall on deaf ears, because I'm not sure many of the homeschooling parents care about this. Obviously, as a public school teacher, I don't have much contact with them, but I did when I ran our Little League baseball program in which some of them would enroll their kids. I realize that this is anecdotal, but in my dealings with them, I found homeschooling parents, by their actions and requests, to be very concerned about their own children, but not about anyone else's, whether they were their children's teammates or kids from other teams. It's natural for parents to care the most about their own children, and there's nothing wrong with that. But hopefully, parents who are concerned about their own kids' education and activities also have some concern for other kids in the community. I think homeschooling parents tend to lack this.

Is God Allowed in Public Schools?

My feelings about homeschooling are very strong because many homeschooling parents are part of the group of public school critics whom I find the most offensive of all. These are the holier-than-thou modern day Pharisees who see public schools as enclaves of evil. They often put it this way: God is no longer allowed in public schools.

The people who promote this message object to the fact that we don't have prayer at the beginning of our school days, the way we did until the mid-1960s. Any reasonably well-informed American knows that we don't have that anymore because we have the separation of church and state in this country. The alternative to this is to have whoever is in power impose their interpretation of their religion on society. If you want to imagine how this might work, just look at what the Taliban did in Afghanistan, or look at Iran or Saudi Arabia.

Many good people argue that the separation of church and state shouldn't preclude prayer in school. Although I'm not sure they're correct, I don't think they are being unreasonable. But I can also remember the discomfort I felt as one of the few Catholic kids in a predominantly Protestant elementary school in Minneapolis in the 1960s when we said a prayer in class that didn't include the sign of the cross. It wouldn't bother me at all now, but it did then. I never felt discomfort when I said prayers with my family at home or in church. I wonder how hard it would be today to come up with a prayer that would not cause some discomfort for some of the students, given all our various religions. I'm not saying that people who believe we should have prayer at the beginning of our day are definitely wrong, but I am saying that those of us who have reservations about that are not necessarily Godless.

But not having school prayers doesn't mean we don't allow God in school. Maybe I'm spiritually confused, but I see God in the way people go about their everyday lives, whether or not they pray in public. Although I would be very uncomfortable leading my first-hour class in prayer, God and my faith are very important to me, and I try to bring that with me to school every day. I think there are a lot of teachers like me in that respect. When teachers go out of their way to help students, I see God in our school. When some kid who "gets it" tries to help some kid who doesn't "get it," I see God. In the last four years in our small school, two of our students have died tragically during the school year. There was an outpouring of love and sympathy for those kids and their families from our community and especially from our school. I definitely saw God in our school then.

My school is fortunate because most concerned parents in our community who care about their kids send them to our school. They send them to our school because they care about them, but also because they care about other people's kids and our community. Am I wrong when I think I see God in many of them? These parents are confident in the values they've instilled in their children, so they don't keep them home or send them to a parochial school because they fear that they will somehow be corrupted by our less than perfect students and faculty. It is their children more than anyone or anything else—teachers, administrators, or all the computers money could buy—that make our school a good place to learn. I see these kids everyday, and I see what they do, and I would bet that there are at least some kids like them in every public school in America. So if some people can't see God in our schools, maybe they should take a closer look.

Changes That Could Make a Difference

Okay, so I've got complaints about almost every reform that's been proposed to fix public education. So what are my ideas? Don't worry: I know what you're thinking, and I'm not going to ask for more money. I have more sympathy than you might think for people who complain about the amount of taxes they pay to improve public education for very limited results. We've seen program after program promising to bring up test scores, or increase the graduation rate, but the results usually seem negligible at best. I am not saying that there are no expensive but worthwhile ideas for improving education, but I can assure you that promoting those ideas is not my purpose. Put away your wallet.

I am convinced that two changes would improve education in America, and if you've been paying attention, you probably already have an idea what they are. The first would involve giving more power to teachers. No, I'm not talking about powers that union-haters find so alarming, like making school policy or forcing school boards to raise salaries. I'm talking about the power for teachers to run their classrooms in a way that allows them to use their training, experience, and common sense to make decisions in the best interest of those students who are really interested in getting an education. My second change would be to grant more power to principals and other administrators to run their schools as they see fit, and to make sure that teachers are doing their jobs.

The major obstacle to giving teachers the power they need to be as effective as they should be is the way education has been interpreted as a property right. As a teacher, I'm all for students having the right to enroll in our school, and I'm all for them having the right to be treated fairly while they are here. But their remaining in our school should be contingent upon their effort and behavior. That should not be a right. The fact that attending school has been treated as such has done more damage to public education over the last forty years than anything else. Philip K. Howard makes that point in his book *The Death of Common Sense,* where he argues that public education should be considered a benefit provided by a democracy, not a property right.[20]

Today we are basically stuck with all of the kids who want to go to our public schools regardless of whether or not they have any desire to learn anything, and regardless of whether they're willing to follow any rules. Laws say that a student should be expelled for bringing a weapon into a school, but for anything else, the twin curses of due process and lawyers make it either impossible or prohibitively expensive to get rid of misbehaving students. If we ever did expel a student in Warroad, our school district would still be responsible for providing him with an education, and that would cost us even more money. In schools like ours, where budget constraints are already forcing cuts in programs and teachers, expelling a student is not an option.

In Minnesota we sometimes have to pay more for troubled students even when we don't expel them. As I write this, our school district is paying $16,000 per year for a student who is in an institution because he got into trouble as a sex offender. That's $10,000 more than the state aid we receive for him. He has never set foot in our school, but his mother moved into our school district, so we have to foot the bill for his "education." We are also paying through the teeth for a student who lived here for a short while and is now in prison because he committed a grizzly rape-murder of an infant. That's right—a rape-murder of an infant, but our school district has to pay because he has a "right" to an education. I don't object to the state trying to educate a juvenile as part of a rehabilitation effort, but please don't tell me that he has a "right" to this, and that

---

20. Howard, P. K. (1994). *The death of common sense.* New York: Random House, 165

our schools might have to make cuts in other programs and personnel in order to provide it.

It's hard to argue against students having "the right to an education," because it sounds so good. If every kid really wanted an education, and if there were no kids primarily interested in seeing what they can get away with, treating education as a property right might work. But in the real world, that just isn't the case. It is clear that the judges who made those rulings, and the legislators who proposed and passed laws that reinforced them, have no understanding of what it takes to run a classroom or a school. I wonder how one of those judges would react if he told someone who was disrupting his courtroom procedures to sit down and be quiet, and that person told him to "shove it." I have the feeling that the judge wouldn't say, "That's okay. You have a right to be here."

Over 200 years ago, Thomas Jefferson wrote in the Declaration of Independence about the rights people are entitled to, and James Madison, Benjamin Franklin, Alexander Hamilton, and several others, when they debated and developed the Constitution, discussed how best to secure those rights. If they had been asked whether those rights should include the right of a student to swear at his teachers without getting kicked out of school, I doubt that any of them would have answered, "Well, sure!"

The most common misconception about education—and it is a misconception that is fed when we call it a right—is that schools educate children. In other words, it is something done *to* them or *for* them. Schools can't unilaterally do it to or for them; the students have to work with us. We can try to motivate, we can present things in different ways, and we can be patient and understanding. We can give them the opportunity. But in the end, students have to decide whether it's something they are willing to do for themselves. As one wise, old principal once said, "We can open the doors, but we can't make them walk through."

Our public schools would be safer places and test scores would soar if, rather than saying to students, "You have the right to an education," we said, "We will give you the opportunity to gain an education, but you will be required to make an honest effort to learn and to follow reasonable rules so we can make that happen." I don't care about students' scholastic aptitudes, race, gender, or social class. I don't care if they are special education students. If they are truly willing, they should be welcome in public schools. If they aren't, then they don't belong there. In other words, they shouldn't have the "right" to simply show up and be there, regardless of what they do.

At our high school and middle school, some students can be removed from class and sent to an alternative learning center, but only the principal can do this. This is helpful, but it just doesn't work as well as if the teacher had the authority to remove the student on his own. For starters, if I am going to go to my principal and request that someone be removed from my class, I had better have documented incident after incident regarding that student. But there may not be many specific incidents worth documenting. The problem may be a student's general attitude displayed in minor actions day after day that make it more difficult for me to teach and for my other students to learn. Also, principals are very reluctant to act on such requests because, as administrators, they understandably start seeing dollar signs and lost state aid whenever a teacher talks about getting rid of any student. As a result, like other teachers, I just put up with behavior that I don't want to put up with. I think it's safe to say that any problem students I have would be more likely to conform to my expectations if they knew that I could act on my own, rather than having to go to the principal.

A teacher needs to be the ultimate authority in his or her own classroom. When teachers are hired, they need to be trusted to use their common sense to decide whether or not students are meeting their obligations. If a teacher determines that a particular student is detrimental to the education taking place in the classroom, that teacher should have the power to remove the student from the class. If two or more teachers feel compelled to dismiss the same student from their classes, that student should be expelled from the school. Teachers and schools should not have to go through groups of lawyers and judges, and this should not cost anybody thousands of dollars.

Obviously, unless a student has committed a particularly outrageous act, he should be put on notice and given a chance to change his behavior before being removed from a class. Nevertheless, the teacher should not have to wait for something outrageous to happen, and he should not have to leave a paper trail before taking action. Students who continually push limits to see what they can get away with, and kids who are constant irritants in the classroom, should not be tolerated. Students who continually fail to do their assignments should also be subject to dismissal, as should students who are habitually absent. If kids are unwilling to work hard enough or show up often enough to give themselves a reasonable chance to pass, why should they be there? What good does it do anybody? The student should receive one warning—perhaps consisting of a meeting with the student, his parents, the teacher, and the principal— and after that, "Good-bye!" An appeal might involve the principal or a panel of teachers, but the process must be simple and inexpensive.

Students removed from individual classes or even from the school entirely wouldn't have to be banished forever. They could be allowed to come back the next year, or even the next semester, if allowing this is practical. If they come back and show that they are really interested in their own education, and that they are willing to follow reasonable rules, great! After all, people grow up, and we should be open to and encourage that. If there isn't a significant change in their behavior, however, they should be dismissed again.

How many students would end up being dismissed if we were able to do this? In a school like ours in Warroad, there would be some, but the number would be small. There are some kids who won't behave no matter what you do, and others who won't try no matter what you do, and they would be gone. But every teacher I've ever talked to agrees that, if we could get rid of just those few hard-core bad apples, there would be a major turnaround among a number of other students. For one thing, the most disruptive and lazy kids would no longer be around to influence anybody else. More importantly, just knowing it is possible to get the boot would have a huge impact on the behavior of students who want to be in school, but who behave badly and make a minimal effort because they know there will be no serious consequences.

As I write this, I have one student out of my 150 whom I would like to remove for behavioral reasons. He doesn't have any kind of diagnosed "emotional disability." For whatever reason, he has decided that he wants to be one of those students who constantly pushes the limits. He is only one student, and he never does anything terribly outrageous, but his removal would unquestionably improve the learning environment of his American history class. There are some students who follow his lead and behave worse than they would if he weren't there, and there are other students who don't like his antics and who would be able to enjoy the class more if he were gone. This student's present behavior warrants dismissal from my class, but he's one of those kids who would probably improve drastically if he thought getting removed from the class was a possibility. As it is now, however, he might get scolded, which he seems to almost enjoy, or he might get detention, which scares him about as much as my Bichon Frisé would scare an ax murderer, or he might get a three-day suspension, which he would view as a vacation.

I also have four students who show no sign of being willing to do the things necessary to pass. That being the case, there is nothing constructive to be gained by their being in my class. One of these students is mildly disruptive, and he is a definite liability. The others also drag their classes down. Making it a real possibility that they might be dismissed from the class is, once again, one of the best things that we could do for these students. This is the one thing that might spur at least a couple of them to make enough effort to pass. As it is now, they simply show up in class and assume everything will be fine. They will keep telling themselves that they will start trying tomorrow, next week, or next month, until finally they realize that it is hopeless, and then they will simply accept their F's, telling themselves that they can always make it up later.

What about those schools that have a lot of disruptive students, and a lot of students who don't do their work? In *The Death of Common Sense*, Howard argues that even in large inner-city schools where people have the perception that almost all the kids are bad, only a relatively small percentage of disruptive students are destroying the education that is supposed to be taking place.[21] But assuming the numbers are larger in those schools than they are in mine, it would be that much more important to get rid of the disruptive students there. As I've said earlier, when you have just a few disruptive kids in a classroom, significant learning can't take place for anybody, so it stands to reason that the more there are

---

21. Howard, *The death of common sense.* 160

in a school, the more important it becomes to free the other students from them. Why should the students who want to learn have to put up with a bunch of clowns who couldn't care less? This concept holds whether we're talking about the richest suburban schools or the poorest inner-city schools.

What about students who need special education, and those who have real problems like ADHD, or emotional behavior disorders? There should definitely be programs for these kids, but again, the students should have to demonstrate a desire to succeed. These kids may have problems that others don't, and we might have to make accommodations for them that we wouldn't for other students, but the onus should be on them to demonstrate that they want to deal with their disabilities as effectively as they can and that they want to be successful.

Teachers need to have the same authority in their classrooms that high school coaches have with their athletic teams. Playing on a high school athletic team has not been interpreted as a right, so coaches can dismiss players if their actions are hurting their team. Because it is clear that coaches have this authority, it rarely has to be used. For example, during my last ten years at Warroad, only two hockey players have been dismissed for failing to live up to our team's behavioral standards.

I can only imagine what it would be like if coaches didn't have this power, and players simply had the right to be there, as they do in a public school classroom. The effort of players in our hockey practices is excellent, and most of that is because they want to be good, but part of it is because players know that a lack of effort won't be accepted. Because of the energy our players put into our practices day after day, our teams and our players get better and better as the season goes on. What would happen if a disgruntled player could simply quit trying, but depend on being able to continue playing on the team because he had a right to be there? What would happen if a player could skip practices, and know that he could return whenever he wanted, and also know that the worst thing that could happen to him would be to have to serve detention? There is no question that our teams and our other players would not be as good as they are. Yet, this is exactly the situation our society has decided to tolerate in our classrooms. Considering this, one has to wonder if our society really believes that academics are more important than athletics.

There are those who think that giving teachers the power to remove disruptive and apathetic students from their classrooms is a radical idea, but it is really just common sense. Up until the late 1960s, this was the way things were done in public schools, and there was never any public outcry that students' rights were being abused. Masses of students were not being thrown out of schools for spurious reasons. In fact, most people believed the system worked pretty well. But then some Supreme Court justices decided to step in and fix what wasn't broken, because some students had been suspended for political protests in their schools. Making decisions to guarantee political and due process rights to students might have seemed reasonable at the time, but I wonder if those justices could have foreseen that their decisions would eventually lead to a high school student in Kansas thinking that he could intentionally vomit on his teacher and get away with it. I wonder if they had any idea how many students they were condemning to worse educations.

If we as teachers ever want to regain the authority we need in the classroom, we are going to have to ask for it. We would have millions of natural allies in the good public school parents who would understand what this means to their own kids' education. Instead of initiating any kind of public debate about this, however, we just talk about our frustrations to each other in the hallways, and that accomplishes about as much as complaining about the weather. Courts have made decisions and laws have been passed, so we lie down and accept them. When it comes to fighting for teachers' rights in dealing with administrators and school boards, we have been fearless. When it comes to fighting for our rights in dealing with disruptive and apathetic students, however, we have been gutless.

Not everyone has been so willing to accept educational status quo. Homeschool parents fight for and get almost everything they want from state legislatures. If they need a law amended, they get it amended. If they need a new law passed, they get it passed. Voucher advocates have gotten the Supreme Court to amend its interpretation of the separation of church and state. They've lost their share of battles in state legislatures and on referendums, but they show no signs of quitting. If those groups can do those things, why do teachers assume that having to put up with kids who don't belong in our classrooms is a situation that can never be changed? I think it's about time that we begin to make some noise about this issue.

Some people think that because the Supreme Court has made decisions on the subject that there is nothing that can be done, but as voucher advocates have shown, that is not the case. In fact, the Supreme Court has overruled its own previous decisions well over 200 times.[22] Writing the Court's opinion for *Planned Parenthood of Southeastern Pennsylvania v. Casey* (1992), Sandra Day O'Connor listed criteria that should be used for overturning precedent. She said the Court must consider whether or not the rule that had been established by earlier Court decisions was workable. It is clear that, for public schools, treating education as a student's property right doesn't work.

If this rule does work, why is it necessary to have voucher systems in some cities so we can remove the most motivated students from the public schools and send them to private ones? Why has homeschooling become such a popular option for parents? Why are we so anxious to label so many schools as "failing"?

Of course, I am a high school teacher, and this is the area of education about which I speak with the most confidence. I am out of my league making recommendations for handling children in kindergarten and first grade. But it is at the middle school and high school levels where we most need to do something to liberate dedicated and "middle of the road" students from non-learners. After all, according to international test scores, it is after fourth grade when our nation's students, as a whole, fall behind students from other nations. This should not be surprising. Disruptive and apathetic students obviously have a greater effect on their fellow students as they get older and peer relationships become increasingly important, and the desire to please adults becomes less important. And I doubt that any other nations are as tolerant of disruptive and apathetic students as we are.

When I've talked to people about the idea of removing kids who don't belong in public schools, I've frequently heard the reply, "Yeah, but what are you going to do with them? Where are they going to go?" To be perfectly blunt, I don't care, but I know where I don't want them!

22. Wilson, J. Q., DiIulio, J. J. (2004). *American government.* Boston, MA: Houghton Mifflin, 423-424

I understand that people don't want teenagers "on the streets" where they can "get into trouble," but if that's what these kids want to do, being in school from 8 o'clock in the morning until 3 in the afternoon isn't going to stop them. For many of these problem students, it's only a matter of time before they drop out anyway. In the meantime, they are detracting from the education of all their classmates, and influencing some of them to adopt irresponsible and sometimes criminal ways. One has to wonder how important this "dragging-down" factor is in some of those school districts with dropout rates of over forty percent.

We may debate about the purposes of public education, but it shouldn't be a baby-sitting service for kids who have no interest in learning anything. We already have alternative learning centers for middle school and high school students, and these could still be used for students who need to be removed from their regular classrooms. I'm not convinced, however, that these kids should continue to be the responsibility of schools, and, in effect, taxpayers, at all.

Dave Kragness, our present superintendent and former high school principal, frequently used to say to parents, "It's our job to educate your kids, but it's your job to send them to school ready to learn." Believe it or not, there were actually parents who would argue with him about that statement. It seems to me that "The Kragness Doctrine" is just common sense, and I think it would make great policy. Children who can't fit into a public school system should become their parents' problems. As was discussed in the previous chapter, homeschooling has become very big in Minnesota, and there are all kinds of instructional materials out there. As far as I'm concerned, those kids are great candidates for homeschooling.

I don't like much about Peter Brimelow's *The Worm in the Apple*, but I agree wholeheartedly with his idea to make the General Educational Development (GED) certification program meaningful, and to remove the stigma from it. A GED is supposed to be equivalent to a high school diploma, but, as Brimelow points out, many employers don't view it as such.[23] As a result, there are a number of kids who want to start making money in the working world, and have no desire to be in high school, but they're stuck there, because they feel like staying is the only way to get that needed diploma.

23. Brimelow, *The worm in the apple*, 224

A lot of kids who are irresponsible in school are irresponsible in every area of their lives. Over the years, however, I have seen other young people who are useless in the classroom, but act like totally different people when they are working at their after-school jobs at various businesses in our area. These are not bad kids, but they aren't buying the arguments about how wonderful and valuable education is. I have no desire to have them in my class so I can make them miserable, and I certainly don't need them there so they can make my other students and me miserable. I'm all for a meaningful GED program that would free them so they could get their high school graduation equivalency and then be able to move on with their lives.

As a teacher, I often feel great frustration in not having more authority in my classroom, so I can understand the frustration principals must feel in not having more authority handling their teaching staffs. I think they should be given more authority, and that means finding some alternative to our tenure and seniority systems. As I stated before, I think the number of truly incompetent teachers out there is much smaller than many education critics would have people believe, but no matter how small the number, school districts should be able to get rid of poor teachers without having to go through the time and expense of a battle against the tenure system that usually make dismissing teachers prohibitive. It seems only reasonable to me that if I want teachers to be able to dismiss students because they're not doing their jobs, then I'd better be willing to allow principals to dismiss teachers if they aren't doing theirs. School districts also should not have to get rid of some of their very best teachers just because these teachers lack seniority when cuts become necessary for financial reasons. I said earlier that most teachers would disagree with me on this issue, but I would say to them the same thing that a retired teacher who became the chairman of the board in a Twin Cities area school district said to me: "As long as teachers have the tenure and seniority systems, the profession will never get the respect it deserves."

If we did not have tenure, however, there could be unscrupulous principals who could release teachers who were high on the salary schedule, not because they were doing a poor job, but in order to save money. There would have to be some sort of safeguard in place to prevent this from happening. I don't like seeing good *young* teachers lose their jobs, but I don't want to solve that problem by having good *senior* teachers lose theirs. I have to believe that the nation that put a man on the moon and won the Cold War can find some alternative to the tenure and seniority systems that would allow us to keep *all* of our best teachers. Regardless of what system we use to pay and retain people, I would still want a union negotiating the overall package for teachers in a school district.

I have to admit that there is an alternative to the ideas I'm proposing that would probably improve education for some students. We can continue moving in the direction that recent court rulings and national policy seem to be taking us, namely toward a full-fledged voucher system. If we do that, there will be concerned parents who will remove their children from public schools in most school districts and use the vouchers to send them to private schools. Removing motivated students will cause the education taking place in many of those public schools to be a little worse than it was before, and this will encourage even more parents to send their kids to private schools. I can envision many school districts getting to the point where almost any parents who cared about their children's education would do this.

Some of these parents would be able to afford to send their kids to first-rate private schools with the help of the vouchers, and those kids would probably get a very good education. Other parents who can't afford that would use the vouchers to pay full tuition at bargain basement private schools and their kids should do okay as well. The instruction at these schools might be a little shoddy since some of the teachers might not exactly be qualified, but that should be offset for students because they would be freed from being in classes with kids who can wreck learning. And let's not forget those parents who are already sending their kids to private schools. Since they'd get a few thousand dollars knocked off the tuition they're already paying, they would get a heck of a deal!

The public schools, on the other hand, would be left with the children of parents who don't care enough about education to move them despite the schools' deteriorating situations. Obviously this would include the most disruptive and apathetic students because, after all, they've got a right to be there. Tragically, the public schools in this scenario would also include some kids who really do have a desire get an education and to better themselves, despite their parents' lack of concern. Actually, I should probably say that these kids *would have had* a desire to get an education, if they were given the chance in a decent learning environment. These are the children who truly would be "left behind."

Albert Shanker, the late president of the American Federation of Teachers, a union leader who was admired even by many conservatives, said it best in a speech he gave a number of years ago. He told his listeners that, "We are about to create a system of choice and vouchers, so that ninety-eight percent of the kids who behave can go someplace and be safe. And we're going to leave the two percent who are violent and disruptive to take over the schools. Now, isn't it ridiculous to move ninety-eight percent of the kids, when all you have to do is move two or three percent of them and the other ninety-eight percent would be absolutely fine?"[24] Although I would slightly amend what Shanker had to say by adding apathetic students to his list, this is the most intelligent statement dealing with education that I've seen from an "expert" during my entire teaching career.

Would vouchers be allowed in my dream education system, where teachers and principals are actually allowed to do the things they should be able to do? Sure. Why not? If public schools were allowed to operate in such a way that teachers were instructing only students with reasonable desires to learn and who behaved well, I don't think there would be much of a demand for a voucher system. But if people were still crying out for the need to have public schools compete with private ones, that would be fine with me. Give us the power to handle our students the same way private schools do, and we will compete with anybody. Bring 'em on!

24. Noll, J.W. (1997).Does school violence warrant a zero tolerance? *Taking sides.* Guilford, CT: Dushkin/ McGraw-Hill, 295

About the Author

Dennis Fermoyle is a graduate of Bemidji State University, and has been a high school teacher in northern Minnesota for thirty-one years. He and his wife, Susan, live in Warroad, Minnesota, and they have three grown children who all attended public schools and have gone on to success in their fields. Fermoyle teaches American History, Advanced Placement American Government, Economics, and Sociology at Warroad High School, and he is a co-head coach of the varsity hockey team. He has been his school district's Teacher of the Year, a local union president, a state championship coach, and president of the Minnesota State High School Hockey Coaches' Association. He earned his Masters Degree in 2001 from the College of St. Scholastica in Duluth, Minnesota.

For more information, or to contact the author, please visit:
www.defenseofpubliceducation.com